World Heritage Series

SANCHI

W9-DIH-391

Text by
Debala Mitra

प्रलकीर्तिमपावृणु

Published by
The Director General
ARCHAEOLOGICAL SURVEY OF INDIA
New Delhi
2003

Special thanks to
M C Joshi, former Director General of the ASI, and to
R S Bisht, B R Mani, Arundhati Banerji and
Hoshiar Singh of the ASI, New Delhi,
without whose assistance this book would not have been possible.
Thanks also to S B Ota and Narayan Vyas
of ASI Bhopal Circle.

Conceptualised by Swati Mitra and Sona Thakur and
designed by Shalinee Ghosh and Krishna Kumar.

Photography by Shalinee Ghosh;
additional photographs by Krishna Kumar (pp. 24-25, 36, 62, 67, 80,
83-85); Sona Thakur (p. 86)

'Recent Excavations' (pp. 24-27) from
Indian Archaeology: A Review (1993-94; 1995-96; 1996-97), New Delhi.

Conceptualised and designed by
Good Earth Publications,
Eicher Goodearth Limited, New Delhi.
Printed at International Print-O-Pac Ltd, New Delhi

Price: Rs 99

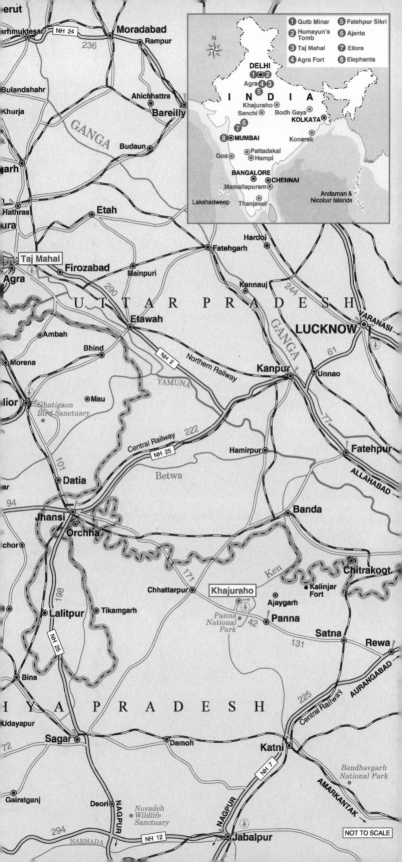

CONTENTS

FOREWORD

The stupas at Sanchi are among the most well-preserved in India. Although not directly hallowed by any incident in the Buddha's life, Sanchi is one of the most popular sites on the Buddhist pilgrimage circuit. Spanning as they do a period from third century BC, the monuments at Sanchi also offer the students of history a wide canvas of Buddhist art and architecture.

The development and conservation efforts at Sanchi are being directed with care to ensure that the atmosphere of serenity that pervades the place is maintained. At the same time, no effort will be spared to ensure that all the amenities and facilities needed by the visitors are in place.

A mini-master plan, currently in hand, aims at achieving effective conservation, improvement and further excavation of the site. According to this integrated development plan, we plan to upgrade the Archaeological Survey of India Site Museum and further enrich it by collecting the pieces of art and antiquities lying scattered at the site. The Government rest-house that was once used by Sir John Marshall, former Director General of Archaeology in India, as his base for his explorations and excavations at Sanchi is being converted into an Information-cum-Interpretation Centre.

With the implementation of these programmes, this complex would be developed into a great hub of activity, incorporating elements of culture, tourism and clean civic life. Our overall endeavour is to ensure that the tourist to India should get physically invigorated, mentally rejuvenated, culturally enriched and spiritually elevated and, on return to his country should feel India within him.

JAGMOHAN
Minister for Tourism and Culture
Government of India

History

*C*rowning the hill-top of Sanchi (in District Raisen of Madhya Pradesh) nearly 91 metres in height, the group of Buddhist monuments presents a spectacular view, even from a distance.

Sanchi is unique in having the most perfect and well-preserved stupas anywhere in India. These monuments record the genesis, efflorescence and decay of Buddhist art and architecture over a period of thirteen hundred years, from the third century BC to the twelfth century AD, almost covering the whole range of Indian Buddhism. This is rather surprising, for Sanchi was not hallowed by any incident in the Buddha's life and the seventh century Chinese traveller, Hiuen Tsang, who so meticulously recorded the details connected with Buddhist monuments, is silent about it. The only early reference to Sanchi is in the chronicles of Sri Lanka, *Mahavamsa* and *Dipavamsa*.

Previous page
Stupa 1
through the
South Gate
of Stupa 3

Below
Stupa 1

These record that Asoka (273-236 BC), well before he became the great Maurya emperor, married Devi, the daughter of a merchant of Vidisa (modern Vidisha), during his halt on his way to Ujjayani (modern Ujjain) as viceroy. Years later when his son, Mahendra, visited queen Devi at Vidisa, she took him up to the beautiful monastery of Vedisagiri built by her. Mahendra had stayed there for a month before he set out for Sri Lanka.

The foundation of the great religious establishment at Sanchi, destined to become an important centre of Buddhism for many centuries, was probably laid by Asoka, when he built a stupa and erected a monolithic pillar here.

Vidisa was the capital of the ancient Akara (eastern Malwa). Several groups of Buddhist monuments sprang up within 20 kms of this place, e.g., at Sanchi, Andher, Sonari, Satdhara and Pipaliya (Bhojpur).

In addition to his marriage with a lady of neighbouring Vidisa, the reason for Asoka's selection of this particular spot may be due to the fact that the hill-top served as an ideal place for a monastery. Its serene atmosphere and seclusion ensured a proper atmosphere for meditation.

Combined with its proximity to the rich and populous city of Vidisa, Sanchi thus fulfilled all the conditions required for an ideal Buddhist monastic life.

The dedicatory inscriptions at Sanchi show that the prosperity of the Buddhist establishment here was, to a great extent, due to the piety of the rich mercantile community of Vidisa. The nearness of the city, its strategic location at the confluence of two rivers, the Betwa and the Bes, as well as on two important trade-routes, resulted in a great overflow of wealth.

This was probably why Sanchi continued to flourish even when the empire of the Mauryas was a thing of the past.

There was a temporary setback following the break-up of the Maurya empire, when the stupa of Asoka was damaged.

Right
The elaborately carved gateway of Stupa 3

The cause of the Buddhist establishment of Kakanaya (another ancient name for Sanchi) was thereafter taken up with feverish zeal by the monks and the laity alike. The religious fervour found its expression in vigorous building activity about the middle of the second century BC, during the reign of the Sungas.

This period saw the stone encasing and enlargement of the stupa of Asoka; the erection of balustrades around its ground, berm, stairway and *harmika*; the reconstruction of Temple 40; and the building of Stupas 2 and 3.

The intense religious aspiration and creative forces continued unabated in the next century as well, when, during the supremacy of the Satavahanas, elaborately carved gateways were added to Stupas 1 and 3.

Early votive inscriptions indicate that the locality was known as Kakanaya or Kakanava in ancient times. Gupta records of AD 412-13 and 450-51, inscribed on the ground balustrade of Stupa 1, refer to the area as Kakanadabota. A later inscription of seventh century AD refers to it as Bota-Sri-parvata. The modern name of an adjacent village, Kanakheda, may be traced to the ancient name.

The Scytho-Parthian and Kushan invasions around the turn of the last millennium and the subsequent establishment of Kshatrapa power in the Malwa region had its repercussions at Sanchi, resulting in a slackening of structural activities here.

Like contemporary Buddhist centres of north and south-east India, Sanchi freed itself, during this period, from the earlier aniconic tradition of Buddhism. However, it did not contribute in any way to the evolution of the Buddha image for which it depended largely on imports from Mathura.

There was a revival of activity at Sanchi during the reign of the Guptas, who, after conquering the Kshatrapas (c. AD 400), provided the peace and prosperity essential for the growth of artistic pursuits. The discovery of a few images made of Mathura sandstone and executed in the early Gupta tradition, proves that Mathura continued, even in the fourth century AD, to meet the demands of the clientele of Sanchi.

Soon after, the local art of Sanchi once more came to the fore, and the four images of the Buddha seated under canopies against the berm of Stupa 1 facing the four entrances belong to this period.

But even in the best days of the Guptas, the figures of the Buddha at Sanchi, did not compare in sculptural merit with their counterparts at such Buddhist centres as Sarnath.

Of the imported Mathura images, mention may be made of the following:
• A seated Bodhisattva image dated to year 28 of the Kushan king Vasishka.
• The pedestal with feet of a standing image containing an inscription dated in the year 22 of Vaskushana.
• The fragment of a pedestal with one foot of an image bearing an inscription which records the installation of Maitreya.
The first two are on display in the Site Museum.

Left
An image of the Buddha seated against the berm of Stupa 1

Temple17

The Gupta period, which ushered in a new epoch in the history of Indian temple architecture, saw a revival of temple building at Sanchi. In Temple 17 at Sanchi, we find one of the earliest Gupta temples noted for its well-balanced proportion, restraint in ornamentation and elegance.

After the glorious days of the Guptas, centrifugal forces once again became rampant. And then came the shock of the Huna invasions, which overran a large part of western and central India. But that occupation was shortlived, as Yashodharman defeated the Huna chief Mihirkula in the first half of the sixth century.

A number of small kingdoms arose, none powerful enough to cover any large part of India, till Harshavardhana (AD 606-647) achieved some sort of political unity in northern India.

His espousal of the cause of
Buddhism brought a fresh lease
of life to that religion. The Buddhist
community at Sanchi prospered
during the seventh and eighth
centuries and several monasteries
and temples were built.

There are a number of Buddha
images in Sanchi executed in the
late Gupta tradition, but they lack
the charm and grace of their
prototypes elsewhere and are
almost lifeless and mechanical.

After the death of Harshavardhana,
northern India once more became
prey to the ambitions of different
dynasties. But Sanchi does not
seem to have been affected by these
political changes, as the existence
of a number of medieval
monasteries and temples testifies
to a period of continued prosperity.

Temple 45, for example, which is now completely bereft of its original splendour, has the same architectural pompousness and exuberance of decoration that characterises other contemporary north Indian architecture. From the discovery of images like Vajrasattva and Marichi, it is abundantly clear that Vajrayana Buddhism did extend its roots here as well.

It is not known how the end came to the Buddhist establishment at Sanchi. No Buddhist monument can be assigned to the thirteenth century AD, though a number of Brahmanical plaques containing representations of Vishnu, Ganesa and Mahishasuramardini, datable to this period have been excavated. These can be seen in the Site Museum.

We do not know if the Buddhists deserted the place or gradually lost the vital force required to maintain their individuality in the face of the all-absorbing force of Brahmanism, which was one of the potent causes of the extinction of Buddhism in the land of its birth.

Temple 45, now bereft of its original splendour

Exploration and Preservation

*F*rom the fourteenth century onward, Sanchi was left deserted and unnoticed. It came into public notice only in 1818 when General Taylor discovered the ruins, of which Stupas 1, 2 and 3 were found intact. The great interest that this discovery created accounts, to a large extent, for the immense damage suffered by the monuments at the hands of amateur archaeologists and treasure-hunters.

In 1822, Captain Johnson, Assistant Political Agent in Bhopal, opened up Stupa 1 from top to bottom on one side, thus leaving a great breach, which resulted in the collapse of the West Gateway and a part of the enclosing balustrade. Stupa 2 was also partially destroyed.

In 1851, Alexander Cunningham, together with Captain F G Maisey, excavated Stupas 2 and 3 and found relic-caskets within. They also sank a shaft at the centre of Stupa 1, which failed to yield any relics. These operations, coupled with the depredations of villagers and the growth of vegetation, wrought havoc on the stupas. Asoka's pillar, for instance, was broken into pieces by a local *zamindar*, to be utilised as a sugar-cane press.

It was only in 1881, that Major Cole took up the work of repairing and preserving the site. In the course of the next three years, he cleared the vegetation, filled in the breach in the dome of Stupa 1, set up its fallen West and South Gateways and a part of its railing, and restored the gateway in front of Stupa 3.

It is believed that in the course of the restoration of the gateways, the original positions of the top and bottom architraves of the South Gateway and the middle and bottom architraves of the West Gateway of Stupa 1 and the top architrave of the gateway of Stupa 3 were reversed. So, what now appears to be their front were originally their back, and *vice versa*.

Previous page
Main Terrace south of Stupa 1, with Temples 17 and 18 in the background

Left
Stupa 2, before and after conservation
(From Marshall and Foucher, *The Monuments of Sanchi*, Vol 3)

The other monuments, however, were left uncared for, and no attempt was made to expose the structures lying buried under the debris. This work was undertaken by Sir John Marshall, Director General of Archaeology in India, who, between the years 1912 and 1919, restored the monuments to their present condition.

Marshall began by large-scale clearance of the jungle. His work thereafter entailed the excavation and thorough conservation of the edifices. This included the complete dismantling and rebuilding of the south-west quadrant of Stupa 1; setting up of its balustrades and erection of the crowning members; reconstruction of the dome, balustrade and crowning members of Stupa 3; resetting of the out-of-plumb pillars of Temple 18; repairs to the perilously-decayed Temple 45; rebuilding of the retaining wall between the Main Terrace and the Eastern Area; the re-roofing and repairs of Temples 17, 31 and 32; and provision of effective drainage. The site was then planted with trees and flowering creepers.

In 1936, Mohammad Hamid excavated the ruins on the hill-slope between Stupas 1 and 2 and brought to light the well-preserved shell of a monastery. Since then, the monuments have received persistent attention and have thus been saved for posterity.

Site Museum

In 1919, a small museum was set up on the hill-top to house the loose antiquities found in the course of the excavations. After India became independent, the monument and the museum, that had hitherto been under the princely state of Bhopal, were transferred to the Archaeological Survey of India. As the building was inappropriate for the proper housing and exhibition of antiquities, a new building was built some years later at the foot of the hill.
Open: 10 am - 5 pm
Closed: Fridays
Entry Fee: Rs 5
(Children below the age of fifteen are admitted free)

Left
Stupa 3 with Stupa 1 in the background

RECENT EXCAVATIONS

Bhopal Circle of the Archaeological Survey of India conducted a small-scale excavation at Sanchi in 1993-94 to expose the buried structures. The south-east side of Stupa 1, near Temple 40, was taken up for excavation. The excavation revealed the remains of a stupa and monasteries or residential structure; and a stone passage running from the south-east to north-west. A patch of burnt earth was traced out in the inner side of a stone structure.

The antiquities found include a silver coin of the Kshatrapa ruler of western India, one pre-Mughal copper coin, iron objects such as nails, arrow-heads, terracotta animal figurines, lamp and beads, stone balls, etc. The ceramic industry included Red Polished Ware, red ware, black ware and other types of historical and medieval pottery. Among the shapes, sprinklers, storage jar, bowls, dishes, *handis* and fragments of spouted vessels were found in large quantities.

The main objective of excavations in 1995-96 was to lay bare buried structures towards the Western Slope and south of the ancient pathway leading to Stupa 2. A cluster of stupas and two apsidal temples were located here on the south of the ancient pathway, which leads from Tank 1 to Stupa 2. A number of other spots were also located containing buried structures.

On the basis of the exploration, it was decided to excavate the area around the stone bowl located to the rear side of Monastery 51, to ascertain its exact location. The area outside the monastery was also excavated to uncover the details of its structural phases and the area where the votive stupas were located on plan.

The excavation conducted around the stone bowl revealed that the bowl was placed on a heap of earth mixed with red *murram*. This heap, in the form of a circular mound, was provided with boulders, arranged all around and one above the other to hold the loose earth.

The well-preserved shell of Monastery 51, with Stupas 1 and 3 in the background

While excavating at the bottom of the elevated portion on the north of the bowl, the lowest course of a wall set in mud-masonry in east-west orientation, measuring about 15 metres in length was traced. Although traces of a few more walls were also unearthed, no clear picture of the structure to which they originally belonged could emerge. However, it is worthwhile to record that a fairly formidable wall running in the north-south direction was traced on plan. On surface, this wall was traced amidst bushes even beyond the pathway leading to Stupa 2.

The excavation also exposed a cluster of twenty-four votive stupas. None of these stupas were found to have more than three basal courses. All these stupas were raised directly over the bed-rock after making the surface plain. Interestingly, all the stupas were within a roughly oblong enclosure. The enclosure-wall comprised unfinished boulders placed directly over the rock.

A part of the enlcosure-wall was found buried. These boulders were arranged in an alignment and were placed vertically. Clearance and excavation at four stupas which were built in a north-south alignment, further down the hill on the Western Slope of the hillock itself were also taken up. All these stupas are bigger in size and were built on square platforms.

The site around Monastery 51 was also excavated. The rear side of the monastery exposed an earlier structure of random rubble-wall set in mud-mortar, comprising in all eleven extant courses, over which the existing monastery stands. There was also found a hiatus between the two structures.

Interestingly, the earlier wall exposed during recent excavations had a regular projected platform, exactly in the middle of the north-south wall, which currently accommodates the staircase on the rear side. Trial-pits, taken along the east-west and north-south arm of the monastery, further confirmed features exposed on the rear side.

The excavation at the ground level also revealed that an apron was provided of rammed burnt brick-bats around the monastery at its working level. The debris just above this layer of brick-bats had a sloping tendency and contained pottery comparable to those found in late-Mauryan, Sunga and Kushan periods. A few pieces of NBPW, sprinklers, inkpot-type lid, fragment of a votive tank, etc., were recovered from the debris.

Detailed analysis of pottery recovered during excavation outside the monastery was taken up to trace the working levels, which might have changed at different periods. A trial-trench was also taken up inside one of the cells of the monastery to arrive at more relevant details. It is now almost confirmed that the monastery had at least three structural phases with the earliest going back to the Mauryan period.

Excavations in 1996-97 were taken up south-east of Structure 8. The excavation revealed that the area had witnessed structural activities in brick between *circa* first century to fourth-fifth century AD, as three monastic complexes were exposed one above the other. These structures were mainly built of hammer dressed-stones in mud-mortar. Interestingly, one punch-marked coin, one hundred and seventy-six silver coins in a hoard of Saka-Kshatrapas and three pre-Mughal copper coins were found from different levels, besides terracotta beads, iron nails, clamps and other minor antiquities.

Left
Detail of gateway of
Stupa 3, before
conservation
(From Marshall and Foucher,
The Monuments of Sanchi, Vol 3)

Monuments
of Sanchi

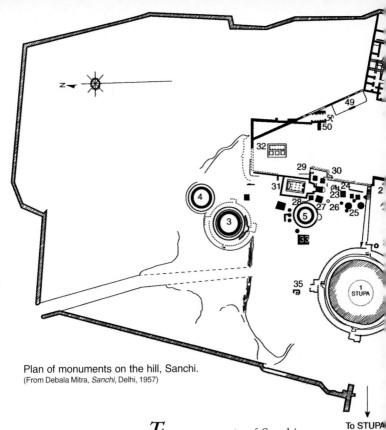

Plan of monuments on the hill, Sanchi.
(From Debala Mitra, *Sanchi*, Delhi, 1957)

To STUPA

*T*he monuments of Sanchi may be divided into two groups, one comprising those situated on the hill-top and the other, the isolated ones on the Western Slope of the hill.

The plateau on the top of the hill is oblong in shape and measures about 384 metres from north to south and 201 metres from east to west. There are three well-defined areas, the Main Terrace, the Eastern Area and the Southern Area, all lying within an eleventh-twelfth century AD stone circuit-wall.

The majority of monuments, numbered 1 to 50 by Marshall, who retained most of the numbers given by Cunningham, are within this walled area. The stepped pathway, leading from the foot of the hill up to the north-west corner of the plateau, was originally constructed by Cole and later extensively rebuilt by Marshall.

Previous page
Temple 18 with Stupa 1 in the background

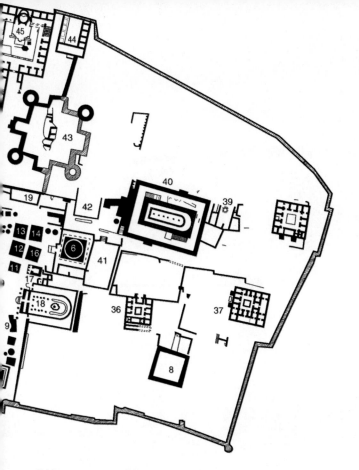

Of late, a motorable road has been
constructed to link the bottom of the
hill with the entrance-gate. Traces of
the ancient road that connected Vidisa
to Sanchi can be seen at Chikni Ghati,
so named on account of the
smoothness of the stone flags due
to constant traffic in olden days.

The monuments on the Western Slope
can be accessed by a path that starts
near the West Gateway of Stupa 1
and leads the visitor downhill, via
Monastery 51 and Stupa 2. Below the
latter, the path joins with the tail end
of an ancient road, paved with heavy
slabs of stone, which begins near
Stupa 7 on the plateau and following
a devious course, joins the alignment
of the present path a little above
Stupa 2. The ruins of a number of
edifices can be seen on both sides
of this ancient road.

32

STUPA 1

*T*he great Stupa as it stands today, consists of an almost hemispherical dome (*anda*), truncated near the top and crowned by a triple umbrella (*chhatravali*), set at the centre of a heavy masonry pedestal within a square railing.

A high, circular battered terrace (*medhi*), approached by a double stairway on the south and meant for circumambulation (*pradakshina*), is built against the base. There is a second stone-paved procession path at the ground-level that is accessible from the cardinal directions through four exquisitely-carved gateways. The diameter of the stupa is 36.60 metres and its height, excluding the railing and umbrella, 16.46 metres.

The present stupa encases an earlier one of about half its dimensions. The earlier stupa was built of large, burnt bricks and mud mortar. It is attributed to Emperor Asoka, on account of the levels of its floor, the inscribed pillar, and the bricks used. The discovery of fragments of an umbrella, made of Chunar sandstone, bearing the typical Mauryan polish, also supports the association of Stupa 1 with Asoka. This umbrella must have crowned the original stupa. The earlier stupa suffered from wanton damage, before the middle of the second century BC, after which it was completely reconstructed.

Stupas originally had a funerary association, being mounds containing the ashes and charred remains of the dead.

Left
East Gateway,
Stupa 1

South Gateway,
Stupa 1

Among the new additions were a stone encasing; a terrace with a double flight of steps; balustrades (ground, stairway and berm); a paved processional path; crowning members comprising a *harmika* in the form of a stupa-shaped stone relic-coffer and an umbrella with a railing; and a stone pavement extending over a large part of the plateau. All this was constructed in sandstone quarried locally or from the neighbouring hill of Nagauri. The plan and form of the Great Stupa as enlarged in the Sunga period is almost the same as it is today.

The casing of ashlar masonry was done by the construction of an encircling envelope a little away from the core and subsequently filling the intervening space with heavy blocks of stone. Both the dome and the terrace were next given a thick coating of concrete and finally finished off with a layer of fine plaster.

The balustrades consist of a series of octagonal (oblong in the case of the *harmika*-balustrade) uprights (*stambha*), with lenticular cross-bars (*suchi*) mortised into them and crowned by enormous copings (*ushnisha*),which are rounded at the top.

The outer faces of the uprights of the berm and stairway balustrades are carved with one complete medallion at the centre and two half medallions at the ends. The medallions are mostly ornamented with motifs of flowers and animals, the latter often drawn realistically.

The ground and *harmika* balustrades are, however, austerely plain. The massive ground balustrade is divided into four quadrants by entrances formed by L-shaped projections of the railing near the cardinal directions. The reproduction of wooden prototypes in the construction of these balustrades shows that the use of stone as building material was relatively new for the builders.

Devotees from all parts of the country sponsored the construction of these balustrades and pavements, which have their names inscribed on them. The elaborately-carved gateways (*toranas*) were built during the Satavahana reign in the first century BC. The offerings of Ananda, a foreman of the artisans (*avesani*) in the court of the Satavahana king, Satakarni are recorded in an inscription on the top architrave of the South Gateway. An extra railing connecting the main balustrade with one of the pillars of each gateway, was also constructed in this period.

The last accretion to the stupa took place after nearly five centuries, some time before AD 450, during the rule of the Guptas. Four images of the Buddha, each seated under a pillared canopy, were installed against the walls of the stupa, facing the four entrances. They are in the *dhyana-mudra*, with an attendant on either side and have elaborate haloes.

The Gateways

All the gateways date to the first
century BC; however, the earliest
to be built was the one on the
south, which is believed to have
been the principal entrance. This
is proved also by the presence of
Asoka's pillar and the landing
with a stairway on that side. The
remaining gateways – North, East
and West – were subsequently
constructed.

The south pillar of the West
Gateway and the middle
architrave of the South Gateway
were gifts by one Balamitra; while
Nagapiya, a native of Kurara, was
the donor of the south pillar of the
East Gateway and the north pillar
of the West Gateway.

The South Gateway is the most damaged, while the North is the best preserved and retains most of its original decorative features, giving an idea of the pristine beauty of the gateways. The builders of these gateways seem to have been essentially workers on wood, ivory and metal – as recorded by an inscription on the west pillar of the South Gateway attributing the decoration (*rupakamma*) to the ivory-workers of Vidisa.

Each gateway consists of two square pillars crowned by a set of four lions, elephants or pot-bellied dwarfs supporting a superstructure of three curviform architraves with spirally-rolled ends. The varied facial expressions of the dwarfs, all represented on the West Gateway are particularly noteworthy; some are groaning under the weight, some bearing it resignedly, while others taking it rather lightly.

The height of the gateways excluding the crowning elements is about 8.53 metres. Between the architraves, separated by four square blocks, are three carved uprights, their interspaces filled with elephant- and horse-riders.

Above
Detail from West Gateway

Below
Detail from North Gateway

Projecting from the abacus of the capitals and supporting the ends of the lowest architraves are graceful bracket-figures of *salabhanjikas*. Between the ends of the architraves are similar though smaller figures, while on the scrolls stand lions or elephant-riders.

A *dharma-chakra*, flanked by *chamara*-bearing *yakshas* and exquisitely-decorated *tri-ratnas*, symbolising the trinity of Buddhism – Buddha, Dharma and Sangha – forms the crown of the architrave. The base of the lowest architrave is relieved with a row of lotuses. The top face of the sill of the gateways is adorned with a medallion at the centre and two half medallions at the ends, with facets in between. The entire surface of the gateways of Stupa 1 is covered with bas-reliefs of scenes and decorations.

Despite a disparity in the standard of workmanship and treatment due to the varying abilities of the sculptors, the carvings are definitely more developed and mature in conception, technique and composition, than those on the balustrade of Stupa 2. They are depicted in more supple, natural and diverse postures, with somewhat freer and unconstrained movements. Though the artist is yet unable to grapple the problem of depth and perspective, the grouping and balancing of figures is done in such a way that they create an illusion of depth and distance. The art is marked by its rhythm, symmetry, decorative beauty and perfect handling of the floral and plant motifs. The Buddhists adopted many popular fables, cults and superstitions and imparted to them the necessary Buddhist complexion.

They even admitted flagrantly amorous scenes on their sacred monuments, which do not quite fit in with the Buddha's teachings. That these gateways, together with the balustrade, were painted is evident from the traces of red paint still visible on the East Gateway and the balustrade flanking it.

The subject-matter of the carvings on the gateways may be broadly classified as follows:

- Scenes from the *Jatakas*
- Scenes from the Buddha's life
- Events in the subsequent history of Buddhism
- Scenes relating to the Manushi-Buddhas
- Miscellaneous scenes and decorations

Below
Through the
North Gateway,
Stupa 1

Page 42
Dvarapala from
North Gateway,
Stupa 1

NORTH GATEWAY

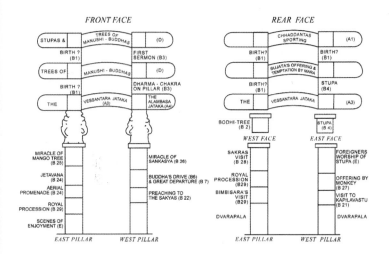

FRONT FACE

| STUPAS & | TREES OF MANUSHI - BUDDHAS | (D) |

BIRTH ? (B1) | FIRST SERMON (B3)

| TREES OF | MANUSHI - BUDDHAS | (D) |

BIRTH ? (B1) | DHARMA - CHAKRA ON PILLAR (B3)

| THE | VESSANTARA JATAKA (A3) | THE ALAMBASA JATAKA (A4) |

EAST PILLAR
- MIRACLE OF MANGO TREE (B 25)
- JETAVANA (B 24)
- AERIAL PROMENADE (B 24)
- ROYAL PROCESSION (B 29)
- SCENES OF ENJOYMENT (E)

WEST PILLAR
- MIRACLE OF SANKASYA (B 26)
- BUDDHA'S DRIVE (B6) & GREAT DEPARTURE (B 7)
- PREACHING TO THE SAKYAS (B 22)

REAR FACE

| | CHHADDANTAS SPORTING | (A1) |

BIRTH? (B1) | BIRTH? (B1)

| | SUJATA'S OFFERING & TEMPTATION BY MARA | |

BIRTH? (B1) | STUPA (B4)

| THE | VESSANTARA JATAKA | (A3) |

BODHI-TREE (B 2) | STUPA (B 4)

WEST FACE | *EAST FACE*

EAST PILLAR
- SAKRAS VISIT (B 28)
- ROYAL PROCESSION (B29)
- BIMBISARA'S VISIT (B29)
- DVARAPALA

WEST PILLAR
- FOREIGNERS WORSHIP OF STUPA (E)
- OFFERING BY MONKEY (B 27)
- VISIT TO KAPILAVASTU (B 21)
- DVARAPALA

SOUTH GATEWAY

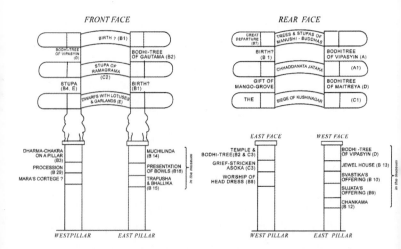

FRONT FACE

| BODHI-TREE OF VIPASYIN (D) | BIRTH ? (B1) | |

| | STUPA OF RAMAGRAMA (C2) | BODHI-TREE OF GAUTAMA (B2) |

| STUPA (B4. E) | | BIRTH? (B1) |

| | DWARFS WITH LOTUSES & GARLANDS (E) | |

WESTPILLAR
- DHARMA-CHAKRA ON A PILLAR (B3)
- PROCESSION (B 29)
- MARA'S CORTEGE ?

EAST PILLAR
- MUCHILINDA (B 14)
- PRESENTATION OF BOWLS (B16)
- TRAPUSHA & BHALLIKA (B 15)

in the museum

REAR FACE

| GREAT DEPARTURE (B7) | TREES & STUPAS OF MANUSHI - BUDDHAS | |

| BIRTH? (B 1) | | BODHITREE OF VIPASYIN (A) |

| | CHHADDANATA JATAKA | (A1) |

| GIFT OF MANGO-GROVE | | BODHITREE OF MAITREYA (D) |

| THE | SIEGE OF KUSHINAGAR | (C1) |

EAST FACE
- TEMPLE & BODHI-TREE(B2 & C3)
- GRIEF-STRICKEN ASOKA (C3)
- WORSHIP OF HEAD DRESS (B8)

WEST FACE
- BODHI -TREE OF VIPASYIN (D)
- JEWEL HOUSE (B 13)
- SVASTIKA'S OFFERING (B 10)
- SUJATA'S OFFERING (B9)
- CHANKAMA (B 12)

WEST PILLAR | *EAST PILLAR*

in the museum

(From Debala Mitra, *Sanchi,* Delhi 1957)

EAST GATEWAY

FRONT FACE

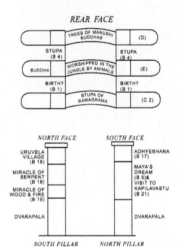

STUPAS &	TREES OF MANUSHI BUDDHAS	(D)
BIRTH?		BODHI-TREE OF MAITREYA
	GREAT DEPARTURE	
FIRST SERMON		BIRTH?
	ASOKA'S VISIT TO BODHI-TREE	

CHANKAMA (B 12)	HEAVENLY
BODHI-TREE (B 2)	
WALKING ON THE RIVER (B 20)	
ROYAL PROCESSION (B 29)	SCENES (E)

SOUTH PILLAR   *NORTH PILLAR*

REAR FACE

	TREES OF MANUSHI BUDDHAS	(D)
STUPA (B 4)		STUPA (B 4)
BUDDHA	WORSHIPPED IN THE JUNGLE BY ANIMALS	(E)
BIRTH? (B 1)		BIRTH? (B 1)
	STUPA OF RAMAGRAMA	(C 2)

NORTH FACE   *SOUTH FACE*

URUVELA VILLAGE (B 18)	ADHYESHANA (B 17)
MIRACLE OF SERPENT (B 18)	MAYA'S DREAM (B 5)& VISIT TO KAPILAVASTU (B 21)
MIRACLE OF WOOD & FIRE (B 19)	
DVARAPALA	DVARAPALA

SOUTH PILLAR   *NORTH PILLAR*

WEST GATEWAY

FRONT FACE

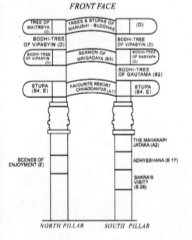

TREE OF MAITREYA (D)	TREES & STUPAS OF MANUSHI-BUDDHAS	(D)
BODHI-TREE OF VIPASYIN (D)		BODHI-TREE OF VIPASYIN (D)
BODHI-TREE OF VIPASYIN (D)	SERMON OF MRIGADAYA (B3)	BODHI-TREE OF KASYAPA (D)
		BODHI-TREE OF GAUTAMA (B2)
STUPA (B4, E)	FAVOURITE RESORT CHHADDANTAS (A1)	STUPA (B4, E)

SCENES OF ENJOYMENT (E)	THE MAHAKAPI JATAKA (A2)
	ADHYESHANA (B 17)
	SAKRA'S VISIT? (B 28)

NORTH PILLAR   *SOUTH PILLAR*

REAR FACE

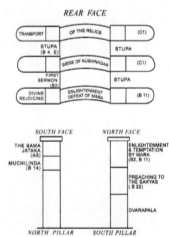

TRANSPORT	OF THE RELICS	(C1)
STUPA (B 4, E)		STUPA
	SIEGE OF KUSHINAGAR	(C1)
FIRST SERMON (B3)		STUPA
DIVINE REJOICING	ENLIGHTENMENT DEFEAT OF MARA	(B 11)

SOUTH FACE   *NORTH FACE*

THE SAMA JATAKA (A5)	ENLIGHTENMENT & TEMPTATION BY MARA (B2, B 11)
MUCHILINDA (B 14)	
	PREACHING TO THE SAKYAS (B 22)
	DVARAPALA

NORTH PILLAR   *SOUTH PILLAR*

Scenes from the *Jatakas*

The stories of the *Jatakas* centre on the previous births of Gautama Buddha. As a Bodhisattva, in the process of attaining 'Buddhahood' or Enlightenment, he is believed to have passed through innumerable births as a bird, beast and man, constantly qualifying for the greatest acquisition of virtues (*paramitas*) like *dana, sila, kshanti, virya, jnana, prajna, bala,* etc. Representations of the *Jatakas* are comparatively rare at Sanchi as compared to Bharhut. The emphasis of the bas-reliefs at Sanchi is more on incidents from the Master's life. Only five *Jatakas* have been identified on the gateways.

CHHADDANTA JATAKA NO. 514

The Bodhisattva, born as a six-tusked elephant (Chhaddanta), lived with his two wives, Mahasubhadda and Chullasubhadda. The latter, in a fit of jealousy, prayed to the Pratyeka-Buddhas that she be reborn as a beautiful maiden married to the king of Varanasi in order to take revenge on Chhaddanta, who she felt was fonder of his other wife.

This *Jataka* forms the subject-matter of three architraves: South Gateway, rear side, middle architrave; West Gateway, front side, bottom architrave; and North Gateway, rear side, top architrave. Of the three compositions, the one on South Gateway is the most expressive and explicit.

In her next birth as the queen of Varanasi, she pretended to be ill and persuaded the king to engage a hunter, Sonuttara, to bring her Chhaddanta's tusks . Though wounded, Chhaddanta took pity on Sonuttara and helped the hunter saw off his own tusks. The queen died of remorse at the sight of the tusks.

The royal elephant is represented here four times; twice near the central banyan-tree, once on the extreme left, where he is shown sporting amidst lotuses, and, last, on the extreme right, standing alone as the target of the hunter's arrow.

SAMA JATAKA NO. 540

The top panel on the south face
of the north pillar of West
Gateway commemorates the
story of the filial love of the
Bodhisattva, born as Sama.

At the top right end of the
panel are the parents of Sama
seated in front of their
respective huts.

Sama is shown near the river
with his pitcher. On the bottom
left, Sama is shown again, this
time wounded by the arrow of
the king, clad as a hunter; a
little to the right is the figure of
the penitent king.

At the top left corner is the
happy reunited group with
Sakra.

Sama (Suvannasama) was
devoted to his aged blind
parents. One day, while at the
river to fill his pitcher, Sama
was shot accidentally with a
poisoned arrow by the king of
Varanasi who was out hunting.
Seeing the plight of the blind
parents, the remorseful king
offered his services to the
couple. The parents' sorrow,
however, moved a goddess, who
brought Sama back to life and
restored his parents' eyesight.

MAHAKAPI JATAKA NO. 407

The Bodhisattva was born as
the chief of eighty thousand
monkeys. He lived with his
retinue off the fruits of a mango-
tree on the banks of the Ganga in
the Himalayas. King Brahmadatta
of Varanasi, wishing to eat the
delicious mangoes, laid siege to
the tree. Finding his monkeys in
imminent danger, the Bodhisattva
jumped to the other bank of the
river. He cut a bamboo-shoot,
one end of which he fastened to a
tree and the other end to his own
waist. The shoot, however, was
not long enough, so he stretched
out and caught hold of a branch
of the mango-tree, allowing the
monkeys to escape by using
his body as a bridge.

His rival, Devadatta, also
born as a monkey, took this
opportunity to kill him by
springing on his body with such
a violent jump, that it broke his
heart. King Brahmadatta, moved
by the Bodhisattva's self-
sacrifice and compassion, gently
lowered his body down. Before
his death, the Bodhisattva gave
an instructive discourse to the
king, who honoured him with
royal obsequies.

The top panel of the front side
of the south pillar of West
Gateway contains a
representation of this *Jataka*.
The top portion of the panel
depicts the monkeys escaping
over the bridge made by the
body of the Bodhisattva and the
shoot tied to his leg, to the rocks
on the other side. The
Bodhisattva's death is not
shown, and, instead, he is
seen seated under the tree,
conversing with the king. In the
foreground one can see the king
on horseback, with his retinue of
soldiers and musicians.

Vessantara Jataka NO. 547

This *Jataka* is depicted in great detail on the front and rear sides of the bottom architrave of North Gateway. The story begins on the right end of the central section of the front side, which depicts the prince on elephant-back behind the battlemented rampart; his gift of the elephant; his leave-taking outside the city-gate after banishment; his departure with his family in a chariot; and his gift of the chariot in the foreground and of the horse in the background. At the left projecting end is the prince, with his son and his wife, Maddi. Maddi is shown carrying her daughter on her hip and all of them are shown plodding through the countryside.

The story continues on the rear side, at the right end of which is depicted the arrival of the family in the forest. The middle shows hermitage life, Vessantara's gift of the children to Jujaka in the absence of Maddi, his gift of Maddi to Sakra, the re-union of the family and the journey back to the capital.

The Bodhisattva, born as Prince Vessantara, was banished from the Sibi kingdom to Mount Vanka as punishment for having donated an elephant, endowed with the power of bringing rain, to the Brahmanas of the drought-stricken kingdom of Kalinga. Vessantara leaves the city with his wife Maddi and children in a gorgeous chariot drawn by four horses.

On the way, the prince gives away first his horses and then his chariot to the begging Brahmanas. He arrives on foot at Mount Vanka, where he and his family live in a hermitage provided by the god Sakra. The prince then gifts his children to the Brahmana Jujaka and his wife to Sakra, disguised as a Brahmana.

Sakra returns his wife to Vessantara and sees to it that he is re-united with his father. Eventually, Vessantara's children are returned to him after his father pays a ransom to Jujaka and they all return to their kingdom.

Alambasa Jataka NO. 523

Here we find the hermitage of Bodhisattva Kassapa. His son, the one-horned Isisinga, who was born of a doe, is depicted with clasped hands, while the doe is seen lying at the feet of the Bodhisattva.

A part of this *Jataka* is depicted at the west end of the front side of the bottom architrave of the North Gateway. Isisinga is shown once in a lotus-pool and again in front of the hermitage.

45

Scenes from the Life of the Buddha

Incidents from the life of the Buddha are prominently represented on the gateways. However, nowhere in Sanchi is the Buddha represented in his human form, his presence being denoted in the form of symbols, such as a caparisoned horse without a rider but with an umbrella held above; a throne; the *dharma-chakra;* a promenade; footprints; and the *tri-ratna.*

The four great events in the Buddha's life were:
- Birth (*jati*)
- Enlightenment (*sambodhi*)
- First Sermon (*dharma-chakra-pravartana*)
- Decease (*parinirvana*)

BIRTH

There is no direct representation of the Buddha's birth, though some have found an allusion to it in the recurring lotus plant, the emblem of miraculous birth. The lotus is shown either alone or with a female figure seated or standing, often being bathed by elephants (similar to the *abhisheka* of Lakshmi in Hindu mythology). The figure is recognised as the Buddha's mother, Mayadevi.

ENLIGHTENMENT

The *sambodhi,* a recurring theme in many of the panels, is shown by a throne (*vajrasana*) beneath the pipal-tree (*asvattha*) where Gautama obtained *bodhi* or Enlightenment. Anachronistically, some panels (for example, North Gateway, rear side, middle architrave) show a roofless structure around the tree, probably built by Emperor Asoka.

In one example (East Gateway, south pillar, front side, second panel from top), the branches of the tree come out through the *chaitya*-windows of the structure.

In the top panel of the east face of the west pillar of South Gateway, the throne with the mark of the *tri-ratna* is placed inside a barrel-vaulted pillared pavilion, above which rise the branches of the *Bodhi*-tree.

This composition probably does not refer to the Enlightenment, but depicts the first temple built by Asoka around the *Bodhi*-tree. This assumption is supported by the panel below, where the grief-stricken figure of Asoka has been identified.

First Sermon

This is represented by a wheel, figuratively set in motion (*dharma-chakra-pravartana*) by the Buddha at Mrigadava (Sarnath). It is placed either on a throne or on a pillar. In the latter case, it is doubtful if it represents the Sermon or the pillar marking the spot of the First Sermon.

The association of Mrigadava is sometimes indicated by the presence of deer. The absence of the first five disciples (*panchavargiya-bhikshus*) among the devotees in all the representations is to be noted.

This is probably because some of these images do not specifically represent the Buddha's First Sermon.

Decease

The *parinirvana* of the Buddha which took place at Kusinagara between two *sala*-trees, is depicted by a stupa. However, in the absence of these trees, it is likely that many of the stupas only represented stupa-worship without any association with Kusinagara.

Panels on the various gateways depicting scenes from the Buddha's life

Other Events from the Buddha's Life

MAYA'S DREAM AND CONCEPTION

Maya's dream and conception is depicted on East Gateway, north pillar, south face, second panel.

After entreaties from the gods of Tushita heaven, the Bodhisattva descended to earth in the form of a white elephant, which Maya, the queen of the Sakya king Suddhodana of Kapilavastu, saw in a dream as entering her body.

FOUR DRIVES

The Four Drives that the Buddha as Gautama took are shown on North Gateway, west pillar, front side, second panel. The theme is summarily treated here, for we only see a chariot, with an empty seat and an umbrella above, coming out of the city-gate. To the left is a riderless horse, which, coupled with the figure of the groom Chhandaka holding an ewer, suggests the Great Departure. Thus two incidents are combined in this panel.

In the course of his drives through Kapilavastu, Gautama came across four ominous sights – an old man, a sick man, a corpse and an ascetic – which impressed on his mind the sufferings of mankind and the bliss of a hermit-life and led to his decision of renunciation.

THE GREAT DEPARTURE

The Great Departure is depicted on South Gateway, rear side, top architrave, east end; and on East Gateway, front side, middle architrave. The treatment of the event on East Gateway is more elaborate.

The four figures of the riderless horse depict the journey of Gautama. On the extreme right is shown the leave-taking of Chhandaka, who is paying obeisance to the footprints of Gautama, below which is represented his sorrowful return with the horse. The *jambu*-tree within a railing at the centre marks Gautama's first meditation under a *jambu*-tree during the ploughing festival in his childhood.

Gautama left Kapilavastu at the dead of night on his horse Kanthaka, accompanied by his groom, Chhandaka, in quest of Perfect Enlightenment. After crossing the Anoma, he sent Chhandaka back with the horse.

WORSHIP OF HAIR-LOCK

Worship of hair-lock is shown on South Gateway, west pillar, east face, third panel.

When Gautama cut off his hair along with the crest-jewel and threw it heavenward, it was borne away by the gods to the Trayastrimsa heaven, where it became an object of worship.

Sujata's Offering

Sujata's offering to the Buddha is represented on North Gateway, rear side, middle architrave. On the extreme left, near the *Bodhi*-tree, can be seen the figure of Sujata holding a tray in her raised left hand and an ewer in her lowered right hand. This incident was also possibly represented on the fourth panel, west face, east pillar, South Gateway (now in the Site Museum).

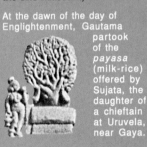

At the dawn of the day of Englightenment, Gautama partook of the *payasa* (milk-rice) offered by Sujata, the daughter of a chieftain at Uruvela, near Gaya.

Svastika's Offering

Svastika's offering is depicted on South Gateway, east pillar, west face, third panel (loose fragment in the Site Museum).

The grass-cutter Svastika offered Gautama bundles of grass to spread on his seat before he took his place under the *Bodhi*-tree.

Temptation and Assault by Mara

The temptation and assault by Mara is depicted on North Gateway, rear side, middle architrave; and on West Gateway, rear side, bottom architrave and south pillar, north face, top panel.

The treatment on the architrave of West Gateway is particularly telling. The *Bodhi*-tree stands at the centre of a hypaethral temple. To the right is the discomfited army of Mara, in flight amidst panic and confusion.

To the left is the solemn procession of happy celestial beings, not given to emotions, the stately and formal group presenting a marked contrast to the host of Mara, full of vigour and action.

When Gautama took his seat (*vajrasana*) under the *Bodhi*-tree, determined not to rise until he had attained Enlightenment, Mara, the Evil One, in order to thwart his purpose, took recourse to tempting and violently assaulting Gautama.

Gautama remained unmoved on his seat and called upon the Earth to bear witness to his right to remain on it. The Earth's answer silenced Mara, who fled with his host. At the defeat of Mara, celestial beings approached Gautama amidst great rejoicing. The same night Gautama attained Enlightenment.

Chankama

The Buddha's *chankama* or promenade is depicted on South Gateway, east pillar, west face, fifth panel (now in the Site Museum); and on East Gateway, south pillar, front side, top panel.

South Gateway, east pillar, west face, second panel (now in the Site Museum) shows the jewel house built by the gods near the *Bodhi*-tree in which the Buddha passed the fourth week in thinking out the *abhidharma*.

After Enlightenment, the Buddha spent four weeks near the *Bodhi*-tree, the third of which he spent in walking to and fro. The promenade is called *chankama*.

49

MUCHILINDA

The Naga king, Muchilinda is shown on South Gateway, east pillar, front side, top panel; and on West Gateway, north pillar, south face, second panel.

The Buddha spent the fifth week after Enlightenment under a goatherd's *nyagrodha*-tree. Next, he went to Muchilinda, where he was protected from the rains by the *naga* king Muchilinda. In both the panels, Muchilinda and his family are shown with the Buddha's seat under the tree.

TRAPUSHA AND BHALLIKA

South Gateway, east pillar, front side, third panel (now in the Site Museum) depicts Trapusha and Bhallika passing through Uruvela. The presentation of the bowls is shown on South Gateway, east pillar, front side, second panel (also in the Site Museum).

On the last day of his seven-week fast, the Buddha, while under the *rajayatana*-tree, was offered food by two merchants, Trapusha and Bhallika, who happened to pass that way with their carts. The Buddha, having no bowl to take the food offered by Trapusha and Bhallika, was at once presented with four bowls by the four guardian-deities (*loka-palas*). One of these *loka-palas* is apparently Indra, as suggested by the presence of Panchasikha.

ADHYESHANA

Adhyeshana is depicted on East Gateway, north pillar, south face, top panel, and West Gateway, south pillar, front side, second panel. This panel on East Gateway is immediately above the dream of Maya and is reminiscent of the gods' earnest request to the Bodhisattva to take birth in the mortal world for the salvation of mankind.

From the *rajayatana*-tree, the Buddha went back to the goatherd's banyan-tree, undecided if he would preach the Truth realised by him. The gods, led by Brahma, exhorted him to preach it for the benefit of mankind. This incident is known as *adhyeshana*.

MIRACLE OF THE SERPENT IN THE FIRE-TEMPLE

The miracle of the serpent in the fire-temple at Uruvela is shown on East Gateway, south pillar, north face, second panel.

In order to convert the three Kasyapa brothers – hermits with matted hair (*jatila*) – who were living with a large number of disciples at Uruvela, the Buddha performed various miracles, one of which was his victory over a serpent. He took residence in a fire-temple that no one ventured to enter as it was inhabited by a venomous serpent. The Buddha overcame the creature, which then crawled into his begging bowl.

MIRACLE OF WOOD AND FIRE AT URUVELA

East Gateway, south pillar, north face, third panel.

After the Buddha's victory over the serpent, a sacrifice was arranged by the ascetics. But, without the Buddha's permission, wood could not be split and a fire could not be lit; oblation could, therefore, not be offered.

BUDDHA WALKING ON THE RIVER AT URUVELA

East Gateway, south pillar, front side, third panel.

This is another miracle performed by the Buddha when he walked over the Nairanjana, then in flood.

VISIT TO KAPILAVASTU

Visit to Kapilavastu is shown on North Gateway, west pillar, east face, third panel; East Gateway, north pillar, south face, third panel.

The panel on the East Gateway is more suggestive. At the top is shown the royal procession coming to meet the Buddha, below which are the aerial promenade and the astonished spectators. On the extreme bottom left, is a banyan-tree symbolising the Buddha's residence at the Nyagrodharama.

At the earnest request of his father Suddhodana, the Buddha, after seven years of his *mahabhinishkramana*, paid a visit to Kapilavastu. The Sakyas, with King Suddhodana at their head, came in a procession to meet him and his disciples, who later took their residence at the banyan-park presented by Suddhodana. To curb the pride of the Sakyas, the Buddha performed a miracle by walking in the air; this made them, and King Suddhodana, prostrate before him.

BUDDHA PREACHING TO THE SAKYAS IN THE NYAGRODHARAMA

North Gateway, west pillar, front side, third panel; West Gateway, south pillar, north face, second panel.

BUDDHA'S RESIDENCE AT JETAVANA

North Gateway, east pillar, front side, second panel. The three favourite residences of the Buddha – Gandha-kuti, Kosamba-kuti and Karori-kuti at Jetavana – are shown in the panel.

Anathapindika, a wealthy merchant of Sravasti, became a convert to Buddhism. In order to present a monastery to the Buddha, he purchased the park of Prince Jeta by paying as many gold coins as would cover the ground.

MIRACLE OF SRAVASTI

North Gateway, east pillar, front side, third panel and North Gateway, east pillar, front side, first panel. In the second panel, the Buddha is seated under the mango-tree, delivering a sermon to King Prasenajit and the courtiers.

In order to confound the six heretical teachers, the Buddha performed a number of miraculous feats in the presence of King Prasenajit, the teachers and a huge crowd. One of them was his creation of a road in the air, which he ascended. On the same occasion, the Buddha caused a mango-tree to grow.

MIRACLE OF SANKASYA

North Gateway, west pillar, front side, top panel

Following the Miracle of Sravasti, the Buddha vanished and went to the Trayastrimsa heaven to expound the *abhidharma* to his mother. After staying there for three months, he descended by a staircase at Sankasya, accompanied by Brahma and Sakra.

OFFERING OF HONEY BY A MONKEY

North Gateway, west pillar, east face, second panel.

The spontaneous offering of honey to the Buddha by a monkey at Vaishali is regarded as one of the eight important events of the Buddha's life.

SAKRA'S VISIT

North Gateway, east pillar, west face, top panel; probably West Gateway, south pillar, front side, third panel.

Sakra, accompanied by his harpist Panchasikha, visited the Buddha at the Indrasaila cave near Rajagriha.

ROYAL PROCESSIONS

Several royal visits and processions are depicted on the gateways. At Bharhut, the kings can be identified from inscribed labels, but, at Sanchi, royal personages have been identified on the basis of the venue of the adjoining scenes.

The procession on the fourth panel on the front side of the east pillar of North Gateway, showing episodes at Sravasti, is regarded as that of King Prasenajit of Sravasti coming out of the city to meet the Buddha. Again, the panel on the west face of the same pillar of North Gateway, immediately below Sakra's visit to the Buddha at Indrasaila cave, is taken to refer to the king of Rajagriha proceeding towards Venuvana, depicted below.

Events in the Subsequent History of Buddhism

SIEGE OF KUSINAGARA AND TRANSPORT OF RELICS

South Gateway, rear side, bottom architrave; West Gateway, rear side, top and middle architraves. Actual fight, which is not vouchsafed by the *Mahaparinibbana-suttanta*, is shown on South Gateway.

The Buddha attained his *parinirvana* at Kusinagara, the capital of the Mallas, who took possession of the bone-relics after his cremation. Now, seven claimants, namely Ajatasatru of Rajagriha, the Sakyas of Kapilavastu, the Bulis of Allakappa, the Koliyas of Ramagrama, the Mallas of Pava, the Lichchhavis of Vaisali and a Brahmana of Vethadvipa, demanded portions of the relics. The Mallas, at first unwilling to share the relics, were brought to reason by the wise Drona, who divided the remains into eight portions and thus averted imminent strife. The claimants returned to their respective lands with their shares and erected stupas over them. Thus came into existence eight relic-stupas.

STUPA OF RAMAGRAMA

South Gateway, front side, middle architrave. To the right of the stupa is Asoka with his retinue, and to the left are the *nagas* with their families.

Of the eight original stupas, Asoka is said to have opened up seven with the intention of distributing the relics contained therein among the innumerable stupas he erected. He, however, failed to secure the relics from the stupa of Ramagrama, zealously guarded and worshipped by the *nagas*.

ASOKA'S VISIT TO THE BODHI-TREE

East Gateway, front side, bottom architrave. The top and the second panels of the east face of the west pillar of South Gateway show respectively the branches of the *Bodhi*-tree rising above a barrel-vaulted temple enshrining the *tri-ratnas* and a distressed Asoka, supported by two queens. The composition on the architrave of East Gateway is quite elaborate. A circular hypaethral pillared structure with open sides enclosing the *Bodhi*-tree with *vajrasana* at its base is seen at the centre. Accompanied by his queen and the full complement of a royal retinue, Asoka is seen twice, once wearily descending from his elephant and, the second time, proceeding towards the structure with clasped hands.

Asoka's visit to Sambodhi is known from his own inscription. The *Divyavadana* refers to the withering of the *Bodhi*-tree through the machination of Tishyarakshita, queen of Asoka, jealous of her husband's inordinate attachment to the tree. This nearly broke the emperor's heart, who, however, succeeded in restoring the tree to its original splendour. Asoka is credited with the construction of a temple over the *vajrasana*.

Scenes Relating to the Manushi-Buddhas

The symbolic representations of the six immediate predecessors of Gautama Buddha (*Manushi-Buddhas*) along with the Buddha himself, were a popular subject with the artists of Sanchi. These can be found prominently on the architraves of each gateway, often covering its entire length.

The representations take the form of either stupas or *Bodhi*-trees. The trees are all different and thus help in the identification of the individual Buddhas. Vipasyin, Sikhin, Visvabhu, Krakuchchhanda, Kanaka-muni and Kasyapa are respectively indicated by the *patali, pundarika, sala, sirisha, udumbara* and *nyagrodha* trees.

The group is often depicted by alternating trees and stupas; but the portrayal by trees alone is also by no means rare, as we find them on the front side of the middle architrave of the North Gateway and the rear side of the top architrave of the East Gateway.

On the front side of the top architrave (north end) of the West Gateway occurs, along with the group, the *Bodhi*-tree (*nagapushpa*) of Maitreya, the Future Buddha.

Miscellaneous Scenes and Decorations

There are also several reliefs which, though unattributable to any known incident in the Buddha's life, are still of religious significance. Among them may be mentioned the worship of the Buddha as symbolised by the empty throne or stupa not only by human and celestial beings but also by the animal world, as seen on East Gateway, rear side, middle architrave.

In some panels of the north pillar of East Gateway, scholars have recognised the different heavens, glimpses of heavenly life, which were intended to act as an incentive to pious work among the masses.

There are also scenes entirely of a mundane character, depicting men and women given to pleasures and sports. Animals, both real and fabulous, with or without riders, form the subject of a number of decorative panels.

Finally, there are the rich and exquisite floral motifs, treated with great delicacy and ingenuity. Particularly noteworthy are the varieties of the 'creeper of life', which often effectively combines isolated beings like birds, beasts and men into one continuous stream of life. Frequently it appears in the role of a *kalpavalli* (wish-fulfilling creeper), producing jewelled ornaments and garlands. This motif, which, like many others, owes its origin to popular beliefs and religion, was sometimes appropriated by the Buddhists to edify their own faith, e.g., on the east face of the east pillar of North Gateway, where the footprints of the Buddha are carved at the bottom and the *tri-ratna* motif at the top of *kalpavalli*.

OTHER MONUMENTS ON MAIN TERRACE

Stupa 3

Situated about 45 metres to the north-east of Stupa 1, Stupa 3, though much smaller in dimensions (diameter 15 metres and height 8.23 metres excluding the crowning members), was modelled after Stupa 1. It has only one gateway, and its dome, extensively rebuilt, is pronouncedly more hemispherical. Of its ground balustrade, four upright-bases alone are now standing; these uprights have a medallion at the centre and two half-medallions at either ends with three facets in between them.

The stupa, crowned by a single umbrella, was built along with its stairway, berm and *harmika* balustrades in the second century BC, not long after the reconstruction of Stupa 1.

It is known from inscriptions that a single individual participated in the gift of the stairway balustrades of both the stupas. After a century or more, the ground balustrade was added, and this was followed by the erection of the carved gateway, most probably in the early part of the first century AD.

Left
Gateway, Stupa 3

Below
Stupa 3 before conservation
(From Marshall and Foucher, *The Monuments of Sanchi,* Vol 3)

Stupa 3

The gateway is slightly over 5 metres high. Its decoration and constituents are similar in subject and style to those of the gateways of Stupa 1, though the workmanship is definitely inferior. With the exception of the scene carved on the front side of the lowest architrave, which has been interpreted as the paradise of Indra (*Nandana-vana*), where Indra is seated at the centre on a throne under a pavilion surrounded by attendants, the reliefs have their analogues on the gateways of Stupa 1.

The importance of this stupa lies in the fact that the relics of Sariputra and Maudgalyayana, the two foremost disciples of the Buddha, were found by archaeologist Alexander Cunningham enshrined at the centre of its dome on the level of the terrace. Inside the relic-chamber, which was covered by a large stone slab of over 1.5 metres, were two stone boxes with their lids respectively inscribed with the words *Sariputasa* and *Maha-Mogalanasa*. The lids are now in the Site Museum.

Sariputra's box contained a white steatite relic-casket, covered by a thin earthen saucer of lustrous blackware, along with two pieces of sandalwood. Inside the casket were found a small fragment of bone and seven beads, variously of pearl, garnet, lapis lazuli, crystal and amethyst. On the inner surface of the lid was written in ink the letter *sa*, the initial of Sariputra. In Maudgalyayana's box was found another casket, somewhat smaller, containing two small fragments of bone. The lid was initialled in ink with the letter *ma*. The relics were taken away to London.

Other Stupas

Besides these two conspicuous stupas, there are the remains of a large number of other stupas on the Main Terrace around the north-east, south-east and south-west quadrants of the Great Stupa. They are either monolithic or structural. The former, often with the relief of a Buddhist divinity, are portable. None of the masonry stupas, however, is intact, and most survive only up to their plinth. Immediately behind Stupa 3 is Stupa 4, ascribable to the second century BC, which exists only in a heap of loose stones without the trace of any ground balustrade. A coping stone, relieved with an undulating stem containing within its foils lotuses, buds, leaves and birds, was found near the stupa; it might have formed part of the balustrade around the *harmika*.

The relics, along with the caskets, enshrined in the new *vihara* constructed in 1952, do not belong, as is commonly thought, to Stupa 3 of Sanchi but actually are from Stupa 2 of Satdhara, west of Sanchi Cunningham discovered two caskets of pale mottled steatite here. The inner surfaces of the lids of these caskets were inscribed, one with *Sariputasa* and the other with *Maha-Mogalanasa* The dimensions and description of the caskets in the new *vihara* tally with those of the Satdhara stupa.

Below
Remains of a large number of other stupas on the Main Terrace

Stupa 5, to the south of Stupa 3, is remarkable in its having an image of the Buddha in the *dhyana-mudra* on a moulded pedestal built against its southern side. The stupa is built on a circular plinth with narrow courses of masonry and with footings; it is ascribable to about the sixth century AD.

The two small stupas, 28 and 29, are to the east of Stupa 5. Both have high square bases with cornices and footings characteristic of the early Gupta age. Stupa 29 presents interesting features, not only in its having a core of large-sized bricks, but also in its having contained, within a small relic-chamber, a bone-relic along with the fragment of a highly-polished vase of the Maurya or Sunga age, placed in a cup of coarse ware with a second cup serving as the lid. The size of the bricks and the presence of the early vase suggest that the relic was transferred here after the original stupa, which might have been of the Maurya period, had fallen to decay. The group constituted by Stupas 12, 13, 14 and 16, about 61 metres south of Stupa 5, is characterised by square plinths strengthened by footings; it belongs to the sixth-seventh century AD. The stupas are built of rubble and earth, faced with well-dressed courses of stone. Some of them contain relic-chambers.

In the fallen debris of Stupa 12, the relic-chamber of which had been completely destroyed before its excavation, was found the foot and pedestal fragment of an inscribed image of Maitreya. Another image, that of the Buddha in the *dhyana-mudra*, made of Mathura sandstone and belonging to the early Gupta period, was found against the western wall of the relic-chamber of Stupa 14.

Right
Stupa 7 in the background

Immediately to the south of this group is Stupa 6. Its core is built of heavy blocks of stone interspersed with chippings as in Stupas 3 and 4, with which Stupa 6 was contemporaneous. The existing facing of both the superstructure and the plinth, the latter square on plan and provided with footings characteristic of the early medieval stupas of this site, dates from the seventh or eighth century AD.

Stupa 7, about 30 metres to the south-west of the West Gate of Stupa 1, has the same structural features as Stupas 12, 13, 14 and 16. It rises to a height of 2.13 metres and is surrounded by the remains of a terrace, probably of a later date.

Pillars

PILLAR 10

None of the free-standing pillars which can be seen on the Main Terrace is intact. The earliest of them is Pillar 10, erected by Asoka, near the South Gateway of Stupa 1, of which the lower part alone now stands *in situ*, fragments of the shaft are placed in a shed near by and its capital is exhibited in the Site Museum. This round and slightly tapering tall pillar, with a highly-polished surface, though not equalling its counterpart at Sarnath, must have been one of the finest columns by virtue of its magnificent capital. Made of Chunar sandstone both the shaft and the capital are monolithic, and bear on them the imprint of the precision of Mauryan workmanship.

The capital consists of a bell-shaped unfolded lotus surmounted by a cable-necking and a round abacus supporting the forefronts of four lions seated back-to-back. The abacus is relieved with four pairs of geese, each separated from the other by a honeysuckle. Although conventionalised, the lions are endowed with a spirited vitality and dignity. The damaged inscription on the stump records Asoka's threat to excommunicate from the Buddhist church any monk or nun attempting to create schism in the *sangha*.

PILLAR 25

Built during the Sunga period, it stands a little to the south of Stupa 5 and is 4.6 metres high. Its shaft is octagonal below and sixteen-sided above. The capital consists of a bell-shaped elongated lotus, surmounted by a deep, square abacus carved with a balustrade in relief. The crowning member has disappeared. The fragmentary inscription, assignable to the fifth century AD, was incised long after its erection.

PILLAR 26

A poor imitation of the column of
Asoka, it stands a little to the north
of Pillar 25. It is broken, with
fragments lying near the platform.
Dating from the fifth century AD,
it consisted of two pieces, one
comprising a square base and a
circular shaft and the other a bell-
shaped lotus, cable-necking, circular
abacus relieved with unsymmetrical
clumsily-executed birds and lotuses,
quadripartite lions and the crowning
dharma-chakra (now in the Site
Museum). The mutilated inscription
on the portion of the shaft standing
in situ records the gift of a Vajrapani
pillar, two pillars of a gateway, the
mandapa of a monastery and a
gateway by one Rudra.

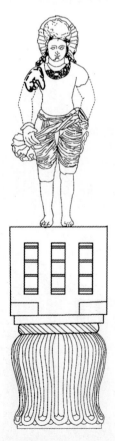

Left
Capital of Asoka
Pillar now in the
Site Museum

Below
Capital of Vajrapani
Pillar, now in the
Site Museum
(Drawings from
Marshall and Foucher,
*The Monuments of
Sanchi,* Vol 3)

PILLAR 35

The Vajrapani pillar (i.e., a pillar
surmounted by a figure of Vajrapani)
apparently refers to Pillar 35 near
the North Gateway of Stupa 1.
Of this massive pillar, only the
standing lower portion of the circular
shaft, the capital consisting of a bell-
shaped lotus, a cable-necking and
a square abacus carved with a
balustrade in relief lying on the
ground and the crowning Vajrapani
have survived.

Vajrapani, clad in a short *dhoti* and
adorned with a jewelled necklace,
heavy ear-rings, bracelets and an
elaborate head-dress of *kirtimukha*
and jewels, is shown standing with
his left hand holding the ends of his
sash. The right hand, which is
broken, apparently held a *vajra,*
a part of which is still traceable on
the right hip. An interesting feature
of this image is its small halo,
pierced with twelve pairs of holes
evenly distributed around the edge
and presumably intended for
receiving the tenons of a metal halo.

TEMPLE 18

This temple is built on the foundations of an earlier apsidal hall of the Maurya or Sunga date. This seventh century apsidal temple originally had twelve pillars, of which nine survive, a pilaster with architraves is also still intact. Temple 18 stands on a raised platform immediately facing the South Gateway of Stupa 1. The platform presumably goes back to the period of the original temple.

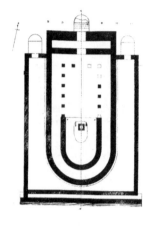

Similar on plan to the rock-cut *chaitya-grihas* of western India, it consists of an apse, a central nave and side-aisles. It differs, in that its apse is encompassed by a solid masonry wall instead of pillars. These 5.18 metre-high, tapering pillars are plain squares with octagonal necking, framed on either side by petals and three-fourth medallions. This is a popular pattern seen in the caves of Maharashtra. Over these monoliths are brackets with rounded edges.

Many terracotta leaf-shaped votive tablets, stamped with the figures of the Buddha, stupas and the Buddhist creed in characters of the seventh or eighth century AD, were found on the floor of the aisles on the eastern side of the apse. The *chaitya-griha* underwent additions in the tenth or eleventh century AD, when the floor-level of the apse was raised by means of stone-filling and richly carved door-jambs were added.

The eastern jamb, decorated with the figure of Ganga with her attendants and bands of floral motifs and human figures, is now in the Site Museum.

All vestiges of the stupa, which once stood at the centre of the apse have now disappeared. A heap of ill-baked terracotta roof-tiles, probably belonging to the original apsidal temple, was found, along with a standard bowl made of polished Chunar sandstone of fine Maurya workmanship, at the foot of the west plinth of the temple.

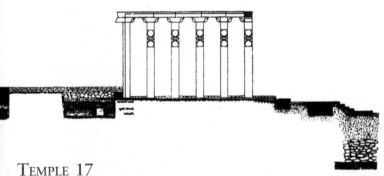

TEMPLE 17

Temple 17 is situated near the north-east corner of Temple 18 and stands on a low moulded basement. It consists of a flat-roofed square sanctum with a portico supported on four pillars in the front. It is a remarkable piece of Gupta architecture, noted for its structural propriety, symmetry, logical proportions and restraint in ornamentation. The capital of the portico pillars bears four lions, each with two bodies. Between the lions, which are at corners, is a tree.

The door-jambs are decorated with vertical bands of foliate and rosette designs. Next to them are two pilasters with bell-shaped lotuses, their shafts similar to those of the pillars. Over the lotuses are block abacii that originally supported detached bracket figures, perhaps of Ganga and Yamuna. The temple is now without any image. In the nineteenth century, Maisey noted in it the lower portion of an image of the Buddha seated on a lotus-throne supported by two lions and inscribed with the Buddhist creed in medieval characters.

TEMPLE 9

The plinth of Temple 9 comprising a shrine and a portico can be seen near the north-west comer of Temple 18. The style and workmanship date it to the early Gupta period.

TEMPLE 31

Situated immediately to the east of Stupa 5, Temple 31 is a flat-roofed pillared shrine, oblong on plan and standing on a high platform ascended by a flight of steps facing south. It contains an image of the Buddha seated on a double-petalled lotus with an elaborately-carved halo around his head. Originally built in the sixth or seventh century AD, the temple was largely reconstructed in the tenth or eleventh century. The platform, the *pancha-ratha* pedestal beneath the lotus-seat and probably the two pilasters similar to those of Temple 18 all belong to the early period. The rest of the superstructure, except the two pillars standing in the middle of the shrine, belongs to the later period.

The pillars in question are of the Gupta period and evidently found their way here from an older building. The image of the Buddha does not fit the original pedestal and was apparently removed from some other temple and enshrined here when the temple was reconstructed.

RETAINING WALL

The high retaining wall, running along the eastern side of the Main Terrace, was built around the tenth or eleventh century, when the accumulation of debris had led to the formation of an artificial terrace (called here the Eastern Area) to its east to a height of more than four metres. The major portions of Structures 19, 21 and 23 and Road 20 lie unexcavated under the terrace.

The *nagi*-figure, standing against the southern face of the platform to the west of the flight of steps, dates from about the fourth century AD. The tenon at its base proves that it had originally been erected elsewhere.

67

THE EASTERN AREA

The stairs against the retaining wall, opposite the East Gateway of Stupa 1, lead to the raised terrace of the Eastern Area.

Monasteries 46 and 47

The path from the stairs leads to two courts, belonging to the same monastic complex which rose on the ruins of earlier monasteries. The lowest floor dates to the Gupta period while the latest buildings were built not earlier than the eleventh century AD.

Monastery 47 is the larger of the two, and has on its south a pillared verandah with a small cell and a long room behind it. On its west is a covered colonnade and in the north a pillared verandah. The verandah leads to an antechamber and a shrine on the western end. In the rear is a corridor and five cells.

Monastery 46 is smaller and can be reached through a doorway in the eastern side of the northern verandah of Monastery 47.

Left
Temple and Monastery 45

Below
Image of the Buddha in a verandah to the south of Temple 45

Buildings 49, 50 and 32

Immediately to the north of Monastery 47 is Building 49 now reduced to its plinth. Contemporaneous with Monastery 47 is Building 50, which is conjectured to have also been a monastery, dating from around the eleventh century AD. Also within the precincts of this complex stands the flat-roofed Building 32, consisting of three small chambers fronted by a common antechamber and an underground cell below the cardinal chamber. The side-chambers have no doors and can be entered only through the windows.

Building 43

The massive Building 43 is immediately to the south of Monastery 47. This massive structure, of uncertain affiliation, is said to be one of the latest constructions at Sanchi. Cruciform on plan, with round bastions at the four corners, it radically differs from all other structures at this site. Excavations have revealed the existence of an early medieval monastery, the floor level of which was at a depth of 3.66 metres.

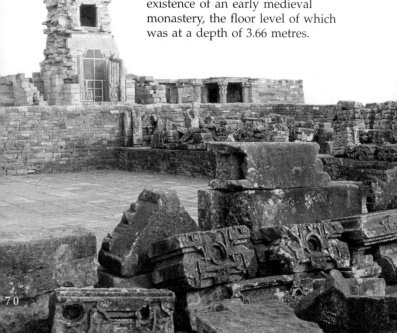

Temple and Monastery 45

Located at the eastern extremity
of the Eastern Area are the ruins
of a towering temple and its attached
Monastery 45. It was constructed in
two periods, of which the earlier one
dates from the seventh or eighth
century AD. This is represented
by small sections of the platform,
the cells on the north, south and
west sides, the pavement of the
courtyard, the plinth of three small
stupas, the kerb at the edge of the
pillared verandah and a solitary pillar.

The eastern cells of the monastery
and the shrine are buried under
later buildings. The verandah, on a
higher level is edged by a stone kerb
composed of alternating oblong and
square blocks, the latter containing
mortise-holes for pillars. Two of the
stupas are reduced to their plinth,
while the upper part of the third,
seems to have been deliberately
stripped off at the time of
construction of a later pavement.

A new temple was built in the ninth
or tenth century AD on the charred
remains of the earlier temple.
A pillared verandah was also
constructed, the level of which
was nearly a metre higher than
that of the courtyard.

Temple and
Monastery 45

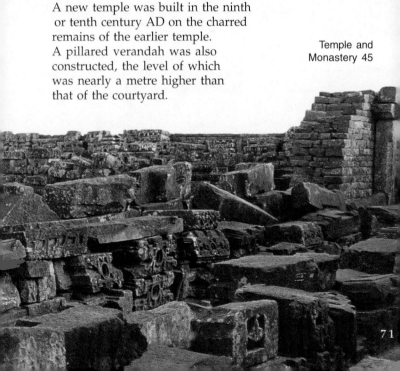

The later temple consists of a roughly square sanctum (*garbha-griha*), surmounted by a hollow spire (*sikhara*), and a narrow antechamber. It is approached by steps from the west. A narrow circumambulatory passage is provided on three sides of the sanctum and antechamber by a high- wall, pierced on the east by two decorated screens.

The ornamented ceiling is carried on architraves supported by brackets set above the corner-pilasters, as well as by independent brackets in the middle of the walls. The pilasters in the sanctum were presumably taken from some earlier structures. Except for the niches in the middle of the sides, the exterior wall of the sanctum is plain.

The surviving images of the *parsva-devatas* in the east and south niches represent respectively the Buddha in the *dhyana-mudra* and Manjusri, seated on a lotus with his *vahana*, a peacock.

The *sikhara* of Temple 45 was once decorated with *chaitya*-windows, *amalaka*-motifs, etc., but none of the original carvings remain. The discovery of a huge but fragmented *amalaka* and a stupa-like *kalasa* conclusively proves that it was crowned in a manner similar to other north Indian *rekha* temples of the period.

Left
Image of the Buddha in Temple 45

Below
Image of Manjusri in the southern niche of Temple 45

The door-jambs and the threshold of the antechamber are richly decorated with figures of animals and floral motifs. The figures of Ganga and Yamuna at the base of the jambs are particularly significant in that they show the adoption of Brahmanical motifs by Buddhists.

On the extremities of the door-sill is a figure of the god of wealth, holding a mongoose in his left hand. In front of the threshold is a moonstone decorated with lotus and conch-shells. The moulded platform in front of the temple is decorated with niches containing some amorous figures.

In the sanctum is enshrined an image of the Buddha in the *bhumisparsa-mudra* on a double-petalled lotus, that is dated to about the tenth century AD. The elongated-oval halo crowning the figure is richly decorated.

Temple 45 is flanked on the north and south by a set of three cells with a verandah, its flat roof supported by pillars removed from earlier structures. The two cells close to the sanctum are provided with richly-carved door-jambs on which are depicted the images of Ganga and Yamuna. One of the door-jambs of the cell of the southern suite contains erotic figures. Nearby, on the verandah, rests a large image of the Buddha in the *bhumisparsa-mudra*.

Building 44

South of Temple 45 lie the remains
of a contemporary structure which
has been reduced to its plinth.
It originally consisted of an
antechamber and a rectangular
hall. The cruciform pavement in
the middle of the hall, with all
vestiges of its superstructure gone,
presupposes the existence of a
stupa. On either side of the hall
are the foundations of tiny cells
of uncertain purpose. In the hall
are two seated figures of
the Buddha.

Left
Door-jamb of
Temple 45

Below
Building 44

THE
SOUTHERN AREA

Temple 40

The track in front of Building 44 leads to the Southern Area. The first structure on this track, beyond Building 43, is Temple 40.

This interesting monument contains the remains of three different periods, the earliest dating to the Maurya age, being in all probability contemporaneous with the stupa of Asoka. It is built on a high rectangular stone platform, 26.52 x 14 x 3.35 metres, and is provided with two stepped approaches on its eastern and western sides. The original structure – an apsidal hall – was probably made of timber. The hall was completely burnt down, perhaps deliberately, some time before the middle of the second century BC, leaving traces of charred wood.

The platform was utilised shortly afterwards for a pillared hall (*mandapa*), of which fifty broken stumps in five rows of ten each still exist. For the erection of the *mandapa*, the platform was enlarged to the extent of 41.76 x 27.74 metres by building a retaining wall at a certain distance all round and filling the intervening space with heavy boulders and worked stones. Three sides of the enlarged plinth have projections of unequal size, the eastern side being still unexcavated.

Left
Temple 40

77

The discovery of numerous pillar-fragments in the debris of the building suggests that there must have been many more that fell with the collapse of the enlarged portion of the platform. Some pillars also contained donative inscriptions in the characters of the second century BC.

Around the seventh or eighth century AD, a small shrine was constructed on the eastern side of the hall. It was in this period, that the row of pillars, square below and octagonal above, was re-installed in its present position. The pillars, though smaller and thinner than those of the hall, belong to the same age, as is evidenced by the votive inscriptions.

Monasteries 36, 37 and 38

These three small monasteries are ascribable to about the seventh century. Built on the usual monastic plan of a square courtyard surrounded by an array of cells with a pillared verandah in front, the entrance, flanked by projecting pylons, lay through the middle chamber of one of the sides.

The existence of upper storeys is indicated by the remnants of steps in Monasteries 38 and 36. Monastery 36 is the earliest of the three, while Monastery 37 is the latest in the group, its plan is more developed than that of the other two. One of the interesting features of Monastery 37 is the additional rooms on its southern and western sides. Monastery 38 was probably built on the remains of an earlier structure.

Building 8

This building, ascribed to the Sunga period, is situated at the south-western corner of the circuit-wall. It has a solid square plinth, standing to a height of about 3.66 metres above the bed-rock to its north. It is approached from the east by a stairway, of which only a few steps at the base have survived. The purpose of the building, and also the nature of its superstructure, are uncertain. During excavations, a large *chandrasila* was exposed near the entrance steps.

Below
Remains of
Monastery 37

THE WESTERN SLOPE

Monastery 51

A modern flight of steps, built against the circuit-wall opposite the West Gateway of Stupa 1, leads the visitor to an imposing monastery built on a ledge of rock, about 7 metres lower than the Main Terrace. This compact and well-preserved monastery measures 33.22 metres from north to south and 32.69 metres from east to west. An interesting feature is that the stone walls are extensively veneered with flat bricks.

The design of the monastery is typical – an open courtyard at the centre with an enclosing verandah and a range of cells behind. The main entrance through the eastern wall is flanked on either side by a massive pylon. The brick-paved courtyard is lower than the verandah. Water from the courtyard was carried off through a drain in the south-west corner.

Excluding the entrance-porches on the east and the comparatively spacious chamber on the west, there are twenty-two cells in all. The four cells on the corners are isolated by verandah-extensions on either side. The central cell on the western side, is fronted by an antechamber formed by breaking the verandah with partition-walls.

Monastery 51 is associated with Devi, a queen of Asoka. One reason for this early dating is the size of the bricks used in the courtyard, walls of the cells and floor of the verandah. However, the evolved plan of the monastery militates against an early dating, and there is a risk in relying on brick-measurements, particularly when the bricks in the monastery were made for special purposes.

Left
Monastery 51

This chamber of Monastery 51 was originally of much larger dimensions and projected, like the chapel of similar monasteries at other sites, beyond the western outer wall. Subsequently, after the collapse of its western wall, the chamber was narrowed down by blocks of masonry, to provide passage for Stupa 2. During the course of excavations, a large amount of charred wood was found, suggesting that the verandah-pillars and the roofs of the cells and verandah had been originally made of wood.

To the south-east of this monastery is an old quarry subsequently turned into a tank. Outside the west gate is a giant bowl, formed by scooping out a large stone boulder. A modern path leads from this spot to Stupa 2.

Stupa 2

Stupa 2 stands on an artificial terrace built against a ledge in the rock, about 320 metres down the slope of the hill. Similar to Stupa 3 in terms of size and contour, it however does not have any gateway. Shorn of its crowning members, berm and stairway balustrades, Stupa 2 appears somewhat bare. But it is compensated to a certain extent by the well-preserved and decorated ground balustrade with four L-shaped entrances. Its double stairway faces east. The palaeography of the inscribed records on the *pradakshina*-balustrade and the style of the bas-reliefs suggest that it was built around the last quarter of the second century BC, though a few reliefs were probably added later.

The posts of the balustrade are ornamented with one complete and two half medallions, with the exception of a few at the entrance which are carved from top to bottom. The theme of the reliefs consists mostly of decorative motifs, Buddhist subjects being a rarity.

The decorative motifs include floral and plant designs, animals – real, mythological and fanciful like stag with elephant's head or fish-tail, *makaras*, griffin, lion with human face, centaur with rider, woman with a horse-head (*yakshi asvamukhi*) – birds, fish, *nagas*, human figures and demi-gods like *yakshas*, *yakshis*, *kinnaras*, etc. Among the floral motifs, the most frequent is the lotus.

Of the animals, elephants and lions are most favoured. Some of the horsemen are shown using stirrups, the earliest known representation of stirrups in India.

Below
Stupa 2

Incidents of the Buddha's life are depicted, including the Departure, Enlightenment, First Sermon and Decease which is represented symbolically by the riderless harnessed horse attended by a groom holding a parasol, the *Bodhi*-tree within a railing having a throne in some cases, the Wheel of Law on a throne and the stupa.

The workmanship of the designs is primitive and contrasts sharply with the more developed art of the bas-reliefs on the gateways of Stupa 1. The carvings are, nevertheless interesting, as they illustrate folk-art in its true indigenous character, unaffected by any sophistication.

In spite of its archaisms, Stupa 2 has the charm of simplicity and decorative beauty. In the treatment of floral patterns it is superb and can challenge any contemporary art. The handling of human figures, however, is singularly crude and archaic, suffering from the 'laws of frontality' and depending on 'memory picture' without any regard for anatomical accuracy and consistency, depth and perspective. A few reliefs at the east entrance, show a more advanced technique and greater skill in modelling.

Thus, in the central medallion on the north pillar, the tall and slender female standing gracefully on a lotus presents a marked contrast to the clumsy and distorted figures seen elsewhere.

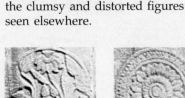

This and similar reliefs were contemporary with those on the gateways of Stupa 1. The stupa itself is no less important on account of the body-relics of a few Buddhist teachers found within its precincts.

Cunningham found within a relic-chamber (which was not at the centre, but 0.61 metres westward) a relic-box of sandstone, 0.28 x 0.24 x 0.24 metres including the lid, its eastern face inscribed with *savina vinayakana aram Kasapa-gotam upadaya aram cha Vachhi-Suvijayitam vinayaka*, i.e., '(relics) of all teachers including *ara* (*arhat*) Kasapa-gota (Kasyapa-gotra) and ara Vachhi (Vatsi)-Suvijayita, the teacher'.

Inside the box were found four small relic-caskets of mottled steatite inscribed with the names of ten saints whose burnt bones were enshrined within. The stone-box and the relic-caskets are also now in the British Museum, London.

The saints were Kasapa-gota, the teacher of all the Hemavatas, Majhima, Haritiputa, Vachhiya-Suvijayata, pupil of Gota, Mahavanaya, Apagira, Kodiniputa, Kosikiputa, Gotiputa and Mogaliputa. Kasapa-gota and Majhima, along with Dudubhisara, Sahadeva and Mulakadeva, are said in the *Dipavamsa* to have been commissioned by Moggaliputta Tissa, after the close of the Third Council during the reign of Asoka, to preach the Law in the Himavat (Himalayan) region.

It is significant that other relics of most of these saints were also enshrined in the stupas at Sonari and Andher nearby.

That all the teachers were not contemporary with one another is proved by the fact that Mogaliputta is mentioned in the Andher and Sonari relic-caskets as a pupil of Gotiputa, himself an heir of Dudubhisara, a colleague of Kasapa-gota and Majhima in the mission.

Thus, in Stupa 2 were entombed the corporeal relics of at least three generations of teachers. Apparently these had their separate resting places before portions were thereof deposited in Stupa 2. This shows that by the second century BC the cult of relic-worship had extended from the remains of the Buddha to those not only of his immediate disciples but also of the later dignitaries of the *sangha*.

Below
Stupa 2

The example set by Asoka in the dissemination of the Buddha's relics was followed in the case of others as well. It is likely and appropriate that the builders of Stupa 2 deliberately chose this lower spot for the enshrinement of the relics of these teachers, as they hesitated to enshrine them on the Main Terrace containing the stupa dedicated to the Master himself and his direct disciples.

A little to the north-west of Stupa 2 and contemporary with it was a pillar with a bell-shaped lotus-capital and a crowning lion. A few fragments of the shaft are now lying on the ground, and the crowning lion is in the Site Museum. Near the pillar are the remains of a ruined stupa.

Practical Information

Arriving in India

When to come
The best time to come to India, especially if you are planning to visit Sanchi, is between October and March. During these months the weather in the plains of north India is pleasant. During the winter months of December and January the day temperature is around 18°C and the night temperature could go down to 5°C.

The summer months of May and June are really hot and the temperature could rise to an oppressive 46-47°C. After the scorching heat, the monsoons arrive around mid-July and the rainy season stretches for a couple of months.

What to wear
India does not have a fixed dress code, but it would be sensible to wear clothes that do not attract unnecessary attention. For travellers visiting Sanchi in winter, light woollens such as a cardigan and a windcheater are usually enough. If you happen to visit Sanchi or Bhopal in the summer, wear loose cotton clothes and cover your head with a hat.

Before coming to India
There are a few things you need to take care of before travelling to India.

Visa
There are three kinds of visas for tourists.

1. The 15-day single/ double-entry transit visa. This visa is valid for 30 days from the date of its issue.

2. The 3-month multiple-entry visa. This visa is valid for 90 days from the date of first entry into India, which must be within 30 days from the date of its issue.

3. The 6-month multiple-entry visa. This visa is valid for 180 days from the date of its issue, not from the date of entry into India.

Visa Extension
It is virtually impossible to get the 15-day or three-month visa extended. Only the six-month tourist visa can be extended. It can be quite a bother to extend it beyond a 15-day period. Avoid it unless there is an emergency.

A 15-day extension on the six-month visa is issued by the **Foreigners' Regional Registration Office (FRRO)** at any of the four metros: **Delhi, Chennai, Kolkata,** and **Mumbai**.

The FRRO office is open on weekdays, 9.30 am to 1.30 pm and 2 pm to 4 pm. A 15-day extension is given only if confirmed air tickets are not available. No fee is charged.

Mumbai
FRRO, Annexe-II Crawford Market (near Police Commissioner's Office)
Ph 022-22621169

New Delhi
FRRO, East Block 8 Level-II, Sector-I R K Puram
Ph 011-26711074

Health
Your health during your travel in India depends on three things: Precautions taken before arrival, day-to-day health care, and efficiency in tackling emergencies.
For travel health, use your common sense and most importantly carry your own first-aid kit, after consulting a doctor.

Especially take care of what you eat or drink. This is the most important health rule.

The tropical sun is extremely strong during the summer months, so guard against sun-stroke and dehydration.

It is advisable to immediately seek qualified medical advise in case any ailment persists for more than a couple of days.

Hospitals
Indian cities have government as well as privately-run hospitals and nursing homes. The government hospitals have modern facilities, but due to a large turnout of patients, medical assistance is slow.

Arriving by Air
The international airports at Delhi and Mumbai provide the most convenient entry-points for the tourist travelling to the World Heritage Site of Sanchi.

Delhi
As the capital of India, Delhi has not only a well-serviced international airport but is also the obvious point from where to make connections for most parts of the country. Delhi airport is called the Indira Gandhi International Airport. It has two terminals: Terminal 1 (for domestic flights) and Terminal 2 (for international flights). Terminal 2 is 19 kms from the city centre at Connaught Place.

Airport Enquiry
Domestic Terminal
Ph 25675121/
25675126

International Terminal
Ph 25652011/
25652021

Airlines Offices
Air India
Upper G F
Jeevan Bharti Bldg
124 Connaught Circus
City Office
Ph 23731225
Fax 23739796
Airport Ph 25696621/
25652050
For Reservations
Ph 23736446-8

Indian Airlines
Malhotra Bldg
F Block
Connaught Place
City Office
Ph 23310517
Airport Ph 140/141/
25675121

Jet Airways
13 Community Centre
Yusaf Sarai
(24 hours Booking Office)
City Office
Ph 26853700/
26562266
Airport Ph 25675404

Sahara India
UG-32
Ansal Chambers I
Bhikaji Cama Place
City Office
Ph 26188512/
26195764
Airport Ph 25675234/
25675357

Mumbai

Earlier known as Bombay, it is extremely well connected by air and rail to most parts of the country. Mumbai airport has two terminals: the Chhattrapati Shivaji Maharaja International Airport, 29 kms from the city centre at Nariman Point, and the domestic terminal, some 6 kms from the international terminal.

Airport Enquiry
Domestic Terminal
Ph 26156500/
26156600/26156009

International Terminal
Ph 28366700/
28318888

Airlines Offices
Air India
Air India Bldg
Nariman Point
Ph 22013031

Indian Airlines
Air India Bldg
Nariman Point
City Office
Ph 22023031/
22023288
Airport
Ph 26156633/
26156943

Jet Airways
B-1 Amarchand
Mansion
Madame Cama Road
Colaba
City Office
Ph 22855788
Airport
Ph 26156666

Sahara India
Unit 7 G F
Tulsiani Chambers
Nariman Point
City Office
Ph 22835671
Airport
Ph 26156363/
26156425

Money
Indian Currency
The Indian currency is called the Rupee. It is available in denominations of 1,000, 500, 100, 50, 20, 10, 5, 2, and 1. One rupee equals 100 paise. Coins in common use are those of Rs 5, Rs 2, Re 1 and 50 and 25 paise. The 20, 10 and 5 paise coins have become redundant in the big cities, but they still have value in smaller towns and rural India.

Credit Cards
Credit cards are becoming increasingly popular in urban areas. All major international credit cards are used, including Visa, Amex, Mastercard.

STD Codes
New Delhi	011
Mumbai	022
Bhopal	0755
Sanchi	07592

Communications
Post Offices
Most small cities have local post offices providing the basic facilities, however in the larger metros they offer a wider range of facilities, like telegraph, fax and a courier service, operating under the brand name EMS-Speed Post. All post offices are open from 10 am to 5 pm, Monday to Saturday.

Telephones
Yellow-painted STD/ISD booths can be found in almost every small town or village today. Most telephone booths remain open till midnight. Some of these also have facilities for sending and receiving fax messages.

Pre-paid Telephone Cards
The state-run MTNL now also offers facilities for buying pre-paid STD/ISD cards, which the consumer can use to make long-distance calls from any ordinary phone. Cell-phone users can also buy pre-paid SIM cards from local network service providers to enable them to use their mobile phones in most Indian cities.

E-mail
Internet and e-mail access are easily available in Bhopal. There are many cybercafes, where for a nominal amount you can access the Net.

Car Rentals
There are several local companies that operate car rental services in most Indian cities, including Bhopal. For self-driven cars, the petrol cost is to be borne by the customer. A valid driving license, passport (for foreigners) or proof of address is required along with a security deposit.

Getting to Sanchi

Sanchi, located in Raisen district of Madhya Pradesh, lies 46 kms from Bhopal, the capital of the state. To reach Sanchi it is advisable to fly or take the train to Bhopal.

MPTDC Offices
(Madhya Pradesh Tourism Development Corporation)

New Delhi
Kanishka Shopping Complex
19 Ashoka Road
Ph 23341187/
23366528

Mumbai
45 World Trade Centre
Cuffe Parade
Colaba
Ph 22187603

Bhopal
4th Floor
Gangotri Complex
Ph 2778383/
2774340
Fax 2774289

Hotel Palash
T T Nagar,
(Near 45 Bungalows)
Ph 2553006/
2577440
Fax 2553076

Arriving at Bhopal
Providing the most convenient gateway for travellers wishing to visit Sanchi, Bhopal is situated on the site of an 11th century city – Bhojapal.

By Air
Daily flights connect Bhopal with Delhi and Mumbai. The airport at Bhopal is around 12 kms from the heart of the city. For latest flight schedules check with your travel agent or the airline offices.

Airline Offices
Indian Airlines & Alliance Air
Airlines House
T T Nagar
Bhadbhada Road
City Office
Ph 2778434/
2770480
Airport Ph 2521789/
2521277

Air India
GTB Complex
T T Nagar
City Office
Ph 263468

Sahara India
3/195 Zone 1
M P Nagar
City Office
Ph 2765242
Airport Ph 2230242

By Train
Bhopal is connected by train to Delhi, Mumbai, Agra and Chennai. It lies on the main line going from Delhi to Chennai. Very few trains halt at Sanchi Railway Station and hence the visitor is advised to embark at Bhopal and travel by road to Sanchi.

Railway Enquiry
The booking office and tourist information counters are on Platform 1.
General Enquiry
Ph 131
Reservation
Ph 2540170

Guided Tours

MP Tourism Offices in Delhi, Mumbai and Bhopal offer various tour-packages to suit all travel needs. For a traveller visiting Sanchi, a day's trip by an air-conditioned taxi from Bhopal to Sanchi and Udaigiri Caves will cost approximately Rs 1,000. In case you need the services of a guide, contact:
MPTDC Office
Ph 2774279/ 2553006.

Road distances from Bhopal
(in kms)

Bhimbetka	40
Bhojpur	28
Sanchi	46
Vidisha	58
Udaigiri Caves	62

Average rack rate in rupees for a standard double room

Ⓐ Above 6000

Ⓑ 4000-6000

Ⓒ 2500-4000

Ⓓ 1500-2500

Ⓔ Below 1500

Where to Stay

Ⓑ **Jehan Numa Palace**
Shymala Hills
Ph 2235107/ 2235104/ 2661101
Fax 2660720

Ⓑ **Noor-Us-Sabah Palace**
V I P Road
Koh-e-Fiza
Ph 2749101
Fax 2749110

Ⓒ **Lake View Ashok**
Shymala Hills
(Opposite TV Premises)
Ph 2660090-96
Fax 2660091

Ⓒ **Residency**
208 Zone 1
M P Nagar
Ph 2556001
Fax 2557637

Ⓓ **Nisarga**
211 Zone 1
M P Nagar
Ph 2555701/ 2555702
Fax 2272701-03

Ⓓ **Ranjit**
3 Hamidia Road
Ph 2534411/ 2535211
Fax 2532242

Ⓓ **Amer Palace**
209 Zone 1
M P Nagar
Ph 2272110/ 2272111
Fax 2575308

Ⓓ **Ranjit's Lake View**
Van Vihar Road
(Near Boat Club)
Shymala Hills
Ph 2660600
Fax 2660321

Ⓔ **Surya**
Hamidia Road
Ph 2741701-3
Fax 2710475

Ⓔ **Palash** (M P Tourism)
(Near 45 Bungalows)
T T Nagar
Ph 2553006
Fax 2553076

Where to Shop

The Chowk and New Market are the main shopping centres in Bhopal. Some of the better-known and more reliable shops in Bhopal are:

Mrignayanee Emporium
23 New Shopping Centre

Handicrafts Emporium
Hamidia Road

MP State Emporium
G T B Complex
T T Nagar

Arriving at Sanchi

By Road

Taxis can be hired from the airport or the railway-station at Bhopal and take about an hour to reach Sanchi. Madhya Pradesh Road Transport Corporation runs frequent deluxe, as well as ordinary, bus services from the Hamidia Road Bus Stand.

These take about one-and-a-half hours to reach Sanchi.

M P Road Transport Corporation
Ph 2540841

Where to Stay

Travellers' Lodge
(M P Tourism)
Ph 266723

Tourist Cafeteria
(M P Tourism)
Ph 266743

Buddhist Guest House
Ph 262739

Heliodorus' Pillar

On the outskirts of Vidisha, 12 kms from Sanchi stands the Heliodorus' Pillar. A *Brahmi* inscription on it records that this Garuda pillar, dedicated to the god Vasudeva (Vishnu), was erected by a Greek named Heliodorus. He was the ambassador of the Greek king of Takshashila (modern Taxila in Pakistan) to the court of King Bhagabhadra of Vidisha. Today the pillar is worshipped by the local people as Khamba Baba.

Udaigiri Caves

Carved into the sandstone hills of Udaigiri, about 16 kms from Sanchi, are a group of twenty Hindu and Jaina rock-cut caves that are outstanding examples of the early Gupta tradition.

An inscription found in Cave 6 indicates that the caves were probably excavated during the reign of Chandragupta II (AD 382- 410).

Among the caves worth visiting are: Cave 4 called Vina Cave by Alexander Cunningham, after the figure of a man carved on the doorway playing the *vina*; Cave 5, which is famous for the Varaha incarnation scene carved on its walls; Cave 13 with its 3.66 metre-long image of Sheshashayi Vishnu portrayed lying on the coils of the primeval snake; and the largest of the Udaigiri caves, Cave 19, popularly known as Amrita Cave after the depiction of the *Amrita-manthan* scene carved above its entrance.

The remaining caves are largely plain.

Further Reading

Burgess, J, 'The Great Stupa at Sanchi-Kanakheda', in Journal of the Royal Asiatic Society of Great Britain and Ireland for 1902.

Cowell, E B, The Jataka, 6 vols., Cambridge, 1895-1907.

Cunningham, Alexander, The Bhilsa Topes, London, 1854.

Hamid, Mohammad, 'Excavation of a Maurya Monastery at Sanchi, Bhopal State', in Annual Bibliography of Indian Archaeology for the year 1937, Vol. XII, Leyden, 1939; and 'Excavations at Sanchi', in Annual Report of the Archaeological Survey of India – 1936-37, New Delhi, 1940.

Indian Archaeology: A Review, 1994-95, 1995-96, 1996-97, New Delhi.

Kern, H, Manual of Indian Buddhism, Strassburg, 1896.

Maisey, F C, Sanchi and its Remains, London, 1892.

Marshall, John (ed.) Catalogue of the Museum of Archaeology at Sanchi, Bhopal State, Calcutta, 1922.

Marshall, John and Foucher, Alfred, The Monuments of Sanchi, 3 vols., New Delhi, 1940 (Reprint, New Delhi 1982).

Marshall, John, A Guide to Sanchi, 3rd ed., New Delhi, 1955.

Glossary

abacus a square or rectangular table forming the crowning member of a capital

amalaka fluted oblate spheroid resembling an amalaka fruit, which forms an important component of a rekha or pidha temple

anda hemispherical dome

apsaras celestial nymphs

apse, apsidal the circular termination of a building

architraves beam or lowest division of entablature which extends from column to column

avesani artisans

berm ledge or narrow open passage

Bodhisattva a being who is in the process of obtaining Buddhahood

chaitya-griha sanctuary

chamara fly-whisk

chankama after Enlightenment Buddha passed four weeks near the Bodhi-tree, the third of which he spent in walking to and fro; this promenade has been called chankama

chhatravali triple umbrella or a series of umbrellas

dharma-chakra-pravartana First Sermon or setting the Wheel of Law in Motion at Sarnath

garbha-griha inner and most sacred chamber of a temple or the sanctum-sanctorum

harmika the railed pavilion on a stupa from which rose the shaft of the crowning umbrella

Jatakas are stories of the previous births of Gautama Buddha, who is believed, as Bodhisattva, to have passed innumerable existences, both human and animal, persistently qualifying himself for Buddhahood

kalasa water-pot, pitcher shaped member in the finial of a temple

kirtimukha decorative motif, showing the grinning face of a lion or any composite creature, from the mouth of which often issue beaded tassels

loka-palas guardian deities

makara a fabulous creature with the head of a crocodile and the body of either a fish or beast

mandapa hall with or without pillars in front of the *garbha-griha*

mahabhinishkramana Gautama's Great Departure from Kapilavastu

mudra gestures of the hand, each of which has a meaning, a symbolic language; for example the *bhumisparsa-mudra* which denotes touching the earth; the *dhyana-mudra* or the meditation pose

medhi high circular terrace

pancha-ratha a temple with five projections, dividing its outer walls

panchavargiya-bhikshus first five disciples

parsva-devatas attendant deities, occupying the niches of the central projections of a sanctuary

paramitas virtues required to become a Bodhisattva

payasa milk-rice

pradakshina path meant for circumambulation

pralamba-pada pose of Buddha seated with feet resting on a lotus

rekha-temple one with a curvilinear tower, which presents the appearance of a continuous line

salabhanjikas tree nymph; motif representing a beautiful young woman

sambodhi Enlightenment

sikhara literally head, denotes a tower or spire, a distinctive feature of North Indian temples

stambha column

stupa originally a piled-up burial mound; constituted the most characteristic monument of Buddhist religion. Stupas were built either to enshrine the body-relics or the personal effects of the Buddha and the Buddhist saints, or to commemorate places and events of religious significance. In course of time, dedication of stupas was considered an act of highest piety, and numerous votive stupas of smaller size were put up around larger Buddhist stupas or shrines.

torana elaborately carved gateway; gateway in the form of an arch springing from two pillars

tri-ratna symbolise the trinity of Buddhism – Buddha, Dharma and Sangha

ushnisha copings; the top row of bricks or stones, usually sloping on a wall

vahana vehicle

vajrasana throne, adamantine seat

vihara Buddhist monastery

yaksha a class demi-gods

Index

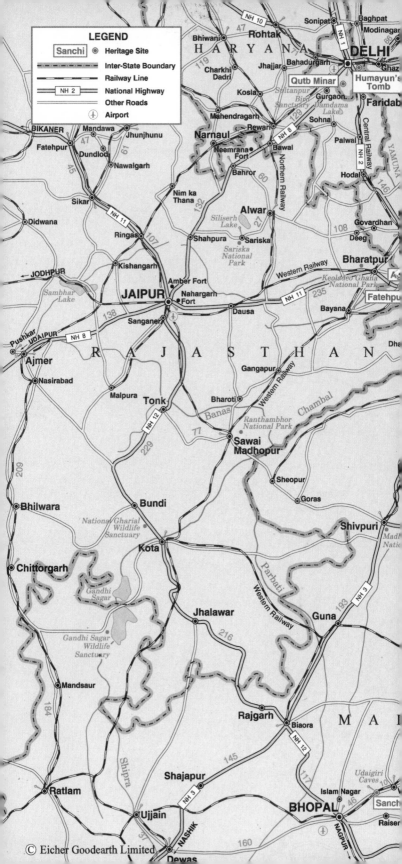

LEGEND

Sanchi ⊙	Heritage Site
	Inter-State Boundary
	Railway Line
NH 2	National Highway
	Other Roads
✈	Airport

HARYANA

Sonipat
Baghpat
Modinagar
NH 10
47
Rohtak
NH 1
DELHI
Bhiwani
119
Charkhi
Dadri
Jhajjar
Bahadurgarh
Ghaz
Kosla
Qutb Minar
Gurgaon
Humayun's
Tomb
Sultanpur
Bird
Sanctuary
Damdama
Lake
Faridab
Mahendragarh
Rewari
129
Sohna
BIKANER
Mandawa
Jhunjhunu
Narnaul
NH 8
Palwal
Fatehpur
47
Dundlod
Neemrana
Fort
Bawal
Hodal
Central Railway
NH 2
146
Nawalgarh
61
Bahror
60
Northern Railway
YAMUNA
Didwana
Sikar
NH 11
Nim ka
Thana
132
Alwar
27
Govardhan
108
Ringas
107
Shahpura
Sariska
Siliserh
Lake
Deeg
JODHPUR
Kishangarh
Sariska
National
Park
Western Railway
BHARATPUR
Keoladeo Ghana
National Park
A
Sambhar
Lake
Amber Fort
JAIPUR
Nahargarh
Fort
Dausa
NH 11
235
Fateh
UDAIPUR
NH 8
Pushkar
138
Sanganer
R A J A S T H A N
Bayana
Dha
Ajmer
Nasirabad
Gangapur
Western Railway
Chambal
Malpura
Tonk
Bharoti
Banas
Ranthambhor
National Park
209
NH 12
229
77
Sawai
Madhopur
Bhilwara
Bundi
National Gharial
Wildlife
Sanctuary
Sheopur
Goras
Shivpuri
Madh
Natio
Chittorgarh
Kota
Gandhi
Sagar
Parbati
Gandhi Sagar
Wildlife
Sanctuary
Jhalawar
216
Western Railway
Guna
193
NH 3
Mandsaur
184
Rajgarh
Biaora
M A I
NH 12
145
Shipra
Shajapur
117
Udaigiri
Caves
10
Ratlam
NH 3
Islam Nagar
46
Sanch
Ujjain
BHOPAL
NASHIK
37
160
NAGPUR
Raiser
Dewas

© Eicher Goodearth Limited